GETTING STARTED

GETTING STARTED

STARTED

How to Set Up Your Own Business

Second Edition

Robson Rhodes

Chartered Accountants

Published in association with the Institute of
Chartered Accountants in England and Wales

KOGAN
PAGE

First published in Great Britain in 1988 by
Kogan Page Limited, 120 Pentonville Road,
London N1 9JN.
Second edition 1990.

British Library Cataloguing in Publication Data
A CIP catalogue record for this book is available from the British Library.

ISBN 0-7494-0124-9
ISBN 0-7494-0125-7 pbk

Typeset by DP Photosetting, Aylesbury, Bucks
Printed and bound in Great Britain by
Biddles Ltd, Guildford

Acknowledgements

I am grateful to my colleagues in Robson Rhodes for their technical help and advice in putting this second edition together and in particular to David Murray of the London Business Support Department.

The forms in this book are Crown copyright and are reproduced with the permission of the Controller of Her Majesty's Stationery Office.

The rates quoted in this book are based on those in the Income and Corporation Taxes Act 1988 and the Finance Act 1989. The Companies Act 1989 received Royal assent on 16 November 1989 and its provisions will be introduced gradually. It will not affect business start-ups.

The Author

David Philip is the Robson Rhodes National Business Support Partner and he has established support units aimed at giving 'hands-on' advice to growing businesses in all Robson Rhodes offices. He lectures regularly on the needs of small businesses and has written several articles on the subject. He is the author of the *Business Start-Up Checklist* which is published by the Institute of Chartered Accountants in England and Wales as an *Accountants Digest*.

Contents

1
Looking At the Project

Are you up to it?

Before carrying out any detailed work on your proposed business you should consider:

- your personal ambitions and the role of the business venture in their fulfilment;
- the aspirations of your colleagues and whether you form a well-balanced team;
- the market for your product; and
- a realistic strategy to exploit that market.

You and your management team

In the early stages of the business, you and possibly a small number of colleagues will be responsible for all aspects of the business, whether it be concluding a major sales contract or ensuring an adequate supply of stationery. Typically, this involves working very long hours and is very stressful. You may suffer numerous disappointments as you come to terms with an uncertain world. You must be convinced that you are able to cope in these circumstances and that your family will support you through any difficult times.

Financiers such as bankers or venture capitalists will not support a business which has inadequate management. Thus, your business should comprise a committed team with complementary skills. In addition, a significant financial commitment from the entrepreneurs is required by most investors.

Setting up in business is very similar to planning for the family's annual holiday. At the outset you choose the area you would like to visit and then research the pros and cons of the various locations by reference to holiday brochures. Having decided this, you look at the prices and pay a deposit.

Then you start planning ahead, buying clothes, arranging for a taxi to take you to the airport, cancelling the milk etc. You would not contemplate the exercise without very careful budgeting and forward planning. How much more important it is to apply the same criteria to setting up a business which is likely to be your sole source of income in future years.

However, for those who are prepared to undertake the planning and control, the financial rewards can be great and the satisfaction in being your own successful boss will be enormous.

The market

You should be aware of the four Ps of marketing:

Product, Placement (distribution), Promotion and Price
Your marketing effort must satisfy each of these four areas in order for the business to meet its sales targets.

It is useful to consider the 'barriers to entry', such as competition, regulations or customer loyalty, which will contrive to lower your sales and reduce your margins. Ideally, your product should be unique and sold in a distinct sector of the market, a 'market niche'. Under such circumstances, entry to the market is relatively easy and you should be able to charge a premium on your rates. Because of lower competition, penetrating an expanding market is generally less difficult than entering a mature one.

From your knowledge of the market you should produce a set of sales projections which are realistic, not only in terms of opportunity but also in the light of your available resources. You should be able to justify your view of the market by reference to independent analyses. Investors are becoming increasingly sophisticated in their investment appraisal and often employ specialists in particular markets or product types.

Your business strategy

You should set realistic objectives for your business and develop appropriate strategies to achieve them. These objectives must be compatible with your personal ambitions and values. Most successful strategies tend to be simple and concentrate on the business's strengths while building an adequate defence against its weaknesses. An over-elaborate strategy which prevents management from concentrating on the key issues is a common failing. So too is failng to define the true nature of your business and its markets. For example, does a manufacturer of home computers serve the market for personal computers or that for executive toys?

Price strategy will be a key issue for the new business. It is surprising how often new companies underprice their products. It is generally unwise to choose a strategy involving high volumes of low-price products. In addition to the manufacturing and distribution problems which could arise, you will be vulnerable to attack from an established competitor by sustained price cutting.

The first project appraisal

If you believe that you can give positive answers to the general questions raised in the preceding sections then you should attempt a written description of your business, a 'business plan', in terms which a financier will understand. In preparing your plan you should invite the assistance and criticism of independent parties and, if necessary, enlist the support of financial consultants.

The business plan should convey the drive, determination and character of the management. It should be stressed that it is your plan and not that of your adviser, and an investor will regard your ability to produce a well-argued plan as a pointer to your other business skills.

The business plan will usually be produced as a first step in raising money from commercial sources. The key elements of the plan, therefore, will be the amount of funds required and the likely return to the investor. Most of your plan will justify your estimates of these two items.

The content of the business plan should include:

- a short (two-page) summary of the business, its management, its projected activities and the funds required; .
- the company's objectives and related strategy;
- the principal activities, products and history;
- the markets, customers and competition;
- research and development;
- the management;
- the basis of operation including suppliers, manufacturing processes and distribution systems;
- major resource requirements;
- financial information, including projected profit and loss accounts, balance sheets and projected cash flow statement with monthly movements for at least two years;
- the principal risks to the business and their likely impact on the funding requirements; and
- the long-term plans of the business.

The financial projections should be as realistic as possible but you should avoid unnecessary detail. The projections must be credible; wildly optimistic forecasts of growth are unlikely to convince investors.

Detailed information which supports the business plan should be included as appendices. These must contain the assumptions which underline the projections and may also include details about major customers and major suppliers, curricula vitae of management and market research data.

Do not underestimate the time taken to raise finance. Bank finance can be arranged relatively quickly, typically within one month. Equity finance, however, may take much longer; time-scales in excess of six months are not uncommon.

Preparing a business plan and raising finance are discussed in greater detail in the following two chapters.

2
Preparing a Business Plan

A business plan is primarily a management tool. It helps you to focus, in a logical and organised way, on the future growth of your company. The business plan acts as a control device against which management can measure achievement.

In addition to its internal benefits, the business plan also serves as a vital document when you need to raise capital (described in detail in the next chapter). A well-formulated business plan will incorporate the following aspects:

An introduction to the business

This two-page summary is the most important part of the document; if it does not create the right impression on the reader, he or she will not read on through the rest of the plan, and the effort put into preparing it will be wasted.

This section should be a concise overview of the business and its products or services, including the background of the business, that is, when it was started and the highlights of its progress, as well as an outline of the key roles of management personnel, previous financing arrangements where applicable and the current ownership of the business. It should also include a statement of its projected activities and the funds required.

The business's objectives and related strategy

This section sets out more precisely the targets that the management have set for the business and the way in which they intend to reach those targets. These targets would include, for example, level of sales, profitability and how much you will take out of the business by way of remuneration.

13

Having set your targets, you must describe how and where you plan to sell and distribute your product or service.

You must explain why customers will buy from you and demonstrate to prospective investors that you understand how your market should be segmented, and that you have the ability to sell and deliver your product or service effectively to the correct targets.

The pricing strategy and policy for your product or service should be explained and compared to your competition. Show how your pricing approach will enable you to:

- penetrate the market;
- maintain and increase market share in a competitive environment; and
- make a profit.

The principal activities, products and history

Before lending you money, a potential source of finance will want to know all about your product or service and the history of your business.

This section will therefore need to explain the product or service, its key features and its benefits to potential customers. It is always useful to include in the business plan brochures or leaflets about your products.

If you have plans for additional new products or services, describe these, and explain how they will meet changing market needs.

The markets, customers and competition

The purpose of this section is to convince the financier:

- that there is a demand in the market for the particular goods or services of your business;
- that you know your product and the niche that it fills in the market-place; and
- that you have confidence in the product or service.

This section should also provide an analysis of existing and potential customers, the market size and trend, and any competition.

When describing the major customers you should mention:

- who they are;
- why they will buy your product or use your service as opposed to those of a competitor;
- when they buy it, whether the demand will be seasonal; and
- what their expectations are for prices, quality and service.

When describing the market size and trends, you should pay particular attention to the current and potential size of the market, and how big it will be in the longer term, ie five to ten years.

Research and development

In many businesses a large amount of funds has been spent or is required to develop a particular product. In this section you should describe the stage of development of the product, costs incurred to date, and the extent to which further finance is required to complete development, test and establish the product in the market-place.

The management

One of the key factors in whether you will reach your targets is the people involved in your enterprise. You should therefore explain how your business's management team is organised and describe each member's primary role, demonstrating how the managers' roles complement each other. Investors are looking for a team with a balance of marketing, financial management and production skills, as well as experience of the product or service you are developing.

A brief analysis of each key manager should be included in which you describe each individual's duties and responsibilities, career highlights, and significant past accomplishments that demonstrate ability for the tasks that will be required.

The basis of operation

A potential investor in your business will also want to know how you plan to operate your business, who your suppliers are and what they supply, alternative sources of supply where possible, manufacturing processes where applicable, including supply and maintenance of plant and equipment, distribution and accounting systems.

This is an opportunity to show that you are in control of the input to your business, and that you have the organisation and capacity to meet the sales targets that you have set. A business which is capable of generating a demand for its products or services, must also be able to supply the demand or the door is wide open for a competitor to fill the gap.

Major resource requirements

It is to be hoped that the preceding sections of your business plan have enthused the potential investor so that he or she feels that you have a business and a management team worth investing in. This is the time to go into greater detail on the finance required, the reasons for it and the time-scale over which the funding is required, so as to set the scene into which the detailed figures of the next section of the plan will slot into place.

Financial information

The business plan should include the following financial information:

- projected profit and loss statements;
- cash flow forecasts;
- projected balance sheets;
- break-even analysis.

Profit and loss statement

The first task of a potential entrepreneur is to prepare a projected profit and loss statement to determine that the business is actually capable of producing a profit. It must reflect your assumptions and plans, which must be stated in detailed notes.

The projected profit and loss statement (Appendix 2) can take various forms, but will usually be drawn up on a monthly basis and will include:

- sales forecasts, both by units (if appropriate) and value;
- estimates of the cost of purchasing the goods and services required, not only to meet your sales forecast but also to build up stocks of your products to service future sales;
- salary levels based on projected manpower levels and costs. Included here would be your own remuneration; and
- expenses: that is, all costs incidental to deriving income, eg rent, rates, light, heat, telephone, stationery.

It is essential not to underestimate the level of your expenses; while it may impress the potential investor initially, it will in due course lead to cash shortages in the business.

When formulating your initial business plan, you should prepare the forecast profit and loss statement for at least two years, preferably longer.

Cash flow forecast

The second step is to prepare a cash flow forecast (Appendix 3). The effective management of cash is a vital part of every business activity. The timing of receipts and payments is very important. Management must be able to anticipate any shortfall and ensure that there are sufficient sources of finance to cover it.

A typical cash flow forecast would include the following:

- amounts receivable from customers for sales. The important element here is not when the sale is made but when the cash is expected to be received, eg 60 days later;
- amounts to be spent on materials linked to the projected purchases and stockholding requirements.
- salary payments including payment of income tax withheld from wages under the Pay As You Earn system and National Insurance contributions;
- expenses: insurance may be paid once a year, rates every month and so on;
- capital expenditure requirements should be phased into the forecast, remembering that heavy expenditure is usually required at the beginning of the project before production can begin and sales can be generated. The capabilities of the capital equipment must be considered in formulating the overall sales plan and related projected requirements and, if necessary, further capital expenditure should be phased into the cash flow forecast;
- the cash flow forecast should include interest payments on borrowed money. This can be a significant expense and should not be overlooked. Any loan repayments must also be included in the cash flow;
- Value Added Tax payments should be incorporated into this forecast as well as income tax or corporation tax payments, as appropriate.

A very careful review is required to ensure that all likely expenses are built into the budget and cash flow forecasts.

It is important to state clearly the assumptions built into your forecasts about things like inflation, interest rates and foreign currency fluctuations that you have made when preparing your forecast and projections. For example, you may assume that the rate of interest on your overdraft is 15 per cent per annum. If, subsequently, this goes up or down, you will know immediately that you may need more cash or alternatively have more than projected. The assumption would be extended to other receipts and payments, such as how quickly you will get your money from your customers and how quickly you will pay your suppliers etc.

Balance sheet

A balance sheet is like a snapshot of where you stand now. It will list your assets and your liabilities and the extent to which you have invested in the business. It is important, when preparing budgeted profit and loss accounts and cash flows, also to project what your position will be in future periods and prepare projected balance sheets (Appendix 4). This will demonstrate to the potential investor the strengths (and weaknesses) of your business in months to come.

Break-even analysis

The preparation of the budgeted profit and loss account will enable you to determine what is your 'break-even point'. In simple terms the break-even point is where the income from your sales is equal to your expenditure on purchases, rent, rates, light and other overheads: in other words where you make neither profit nor loss. This is a very effective management tool even for those with no financial background. For example, suppose, to break even, your sales need to be £10,000 per week. Then sales of £9000 will mean you are making a loss, and sales of £11,000 a profit. In Chapter 8 we give a more detailed analysis of the calculations of the break-even point.

It is always useful to prepare a very 'rough' budget and cash flow to begin with and then start to analyse and refine each figure until you arrive at an acceptable result. For example, you may find that your sales price is too low or that you have underestimated certain overheads.

Principal risks

It is important to understand the dynamics of what makes your business tick. In order to do this you should ask yourself 'what if?' For example, what if sales are higher or lower than predicted? What if I do not collect from the debtors in 60 days? What if a major customer takes his or her orders elsewhere? By calculating the effect of these questions on your forecasts (known as *sensitivity analysis*) you will be in a better position to know what defensive action you can take if a problem arises.

The business plan should go on to describe the inherent risks to which your business is vulnerable and how you intend to monitor and control them. Your financial projections should include the sensitivity analyses mentioned above, highlighting how your profit and cash flow forecasts will be affected by, for example:

- deviations from forecast sales;
- any change in the cost of sales;
- the timing of large expenditure on capital items;
- any possible changes in the pricing policy;

- any changes in the distribution policy;
- fluctuations in interest rates;
- where the business trades outside the UK, any foreign exchange fluctuations.

The long-term plans of the business

This is an opportunity to set objectives for your business in the medium to long term, based on your forecasts and projections in the short term.

Once you have made all your plans, forecasts and projections, and when your business plan has been prepared, you have a document which identifies the level of finance you require. The next step is to determine which of the many sources of finance available is appropriate.

Detailed information

Finally you will need to include in appendices all the detailed information on your business plan. These would include the detailed budgeting schedules, assumptions, details of management, product literature etc. A suggested contents list for a business plan is given in Appendix 1.

3
Financing the Business

Having decided the level of finance you require it is then necessary to determine the structure of that finance and to understand the particular requirements of the financier. Whether finance is required for a start-up, to buy out an existing business, expand the business by increasing the overdraft or on long-term loans for capital purposes, the principles are the same. Most people raising finance for the first time automatically think of their bank and tend to approach their bank manager without really understanding the various types of finance or the fact that there are alternative sources.

Equity/debt finance

A firm's capital can be broadly classified either as (a) equity (shareholders' funds in the case of a company, or proprietor's funds in the case of a sole trader or partnership); or (b) as debt.

Equity
Equity is how much money you and other investors have put into the business. In the case of a company the shareholders cannot, legally, extract their funds from the business except under certain circumstances (eg if the company is wound up or special types of shares are held). While in relation to sole traders and partnerships the funds can be more easily withdrawn, it is not advisable to do so if such an action will be detrimental to the business.

Debt finance
Debt finance is basically the amount of money borrowed by the business where the leader ultimately expects repayment. The period over which such funds are repaid can be short term (eg overdrafts), medium term (eg

loans for three to ten years) or longer term depending on the purpose to which the money is put.

Generally, no interest is payable on equity finance but debt finance is subject to the payment of interest on a regular basis.

The relationship between equity and debt finance is extremely important to the survival of the business and is an area that a potential investor will wish to review in detail. As a very general rule you should work on the basis that no investor would wish to have more money in the business than the proprietor.

Financial stability

If it is to flourish, a firm should have an adequate equity base. This can be measured by what is known as the capital gearing, ie the proportion of borrowed money to equity capital. Every firm is different but it should not be difficult for an individual firm to establish within what range its gearing ratio should normally fall. Thus, the more risky a firm's business, the lower the desirable gearing ratio will be. A balance sheet may have a capital gearing ratio of not more than 1:2, that is, with equity being at least twice borrowings, but this ratio may sometimes be allowed to deteriorate to 1:1 without undue external criticism. However, it might be interpreted as a signal that a further injection of equity is desirable.

The chief dangers of high capital gearing (ie having too much borrowed money in the business) are that earnings may be insufficient to cover interest payments and that cash flow may be insufficient to fund capital repayments. A well-used criterion is whether net trading profits (before interest and tax) cover interest charges at least twice over.

The capital gearing and interest cover ratios just mentioned are not definitive criteria, and much will depend on the efficiency and prospects of the firm. Thus, if the management is failing to maximise the earning potential of the firm's assets, it may be wise to avoid borrowing and instead maintain a high proportion of equity in the firm's capital structure. Similarly, the repayment structure of a firm's existing debt must be considered. Thus, an unbalanced debt structure may be characterised by large borrowings 'locked in' at high interest rates, or by a large proportion of debt requiring early repayment. Until more appropriate terms can be arranged, it would be prudent to maintain a larger than average equity base.

Banks do in fact provide finance to small firms with gearing ratios in excess of 1:1, but it is unreasonable to expect banks to put more depositers' money into a business than the money put in by the proprietors.

To summarise, while the securing of adequate finance can be a major hurdle for any new business, the ability to strike the right balance between shareholders' funds and borrowings can be crucial to its eventual success. The funding of any business should enable it to survive the possible, rather than the planned, outcome.

The next section describes a number of sources of finance, but it is important that a business does not try to use too many sources simultaneously. Difficulties can arise when a large number of lending institutions are involved with a single company, and an enormous amount of time can be spent negotiating and keeping the sources appraised of how the business is progressing.

Types of finance

Types of finance can be categorised into the following broad headings: short-, medium- and long-term finance.

Short-term finance
The term is used here to describe finance for periods of up to three years. Such finance is used mostly for the following purposes:

- to meet fluctuations in the working capital requirements of the business; that is, the cash that is required to meet day-to-day expenditure, such as purchases, wages, overheads less cash received, for example from sales;
- to finance seasonal peaks and troughs in trade;
- for investment in fixed assets with a relatively short working life, such as motor vehicles;
- to act as bridging finance until more permanent finance is arranged.

Overdrafts
A bank overdraft is the most widely used type of short-term finance. Overdrafts, which is the term for flexible, variable lines of credit, are still popular. Legal documentation is at a minimum with these arrangements; interest is often charged at a higher rate than on medium/long-term loans. However, bank overdrafts are repayable on demand, and are therefore not a suitable way to finance expenditure where the benefits from it are in the longer term.

Trade credit
It is usual for a firm to add to its short-term working capital by making use of the trade credit that suppliers extend. However, to make payments

beyond the period stipulated could result in a withdrawal of goods on credit by the supplier.

Customer financing
This method of short-term finance involves a company asking its customers to finance all or part of a contract by way of deposit or advance payment.

Credit factoring
Factoring is another widely used facility whereby the 'factor' purchases the trade debtors of the company for an agreed reward. The advantages here can be improved short-term cash flow and less administrative time spent on credit control.

Hire purchase
Hire purchase is a method of purchasing assets by instalments. After making an initial down payment, and paying regular fixed amounts over an agreed period, a business acquires ownership of the goods. Technically, the financier continues to own the asset until the hirer, at the end of the repayment period, exercises his or her option to purchase.

Leasing
A lease is a means of financing the use of an asset and not its purchase. It is frequently used to finance motor vehicles, office equipment such as computers, photocopiers, telex or facsimile machines, as well as factory plant and equipment. The leasing company retains ownership of the asset and claims any available grant and tax allowance. These are reflected in the rental charge to the user.

Leasing finance may be classified as short- or medium-term finance depending on the length of the lease.

Bill finance
Bills of exchange are a source of short-term money which are used mostly in the export and import trade. A bill of exchange is in effect a form of post-dated cheque which can be sold at a discount for cash. A seller of goods draws up a bill which is then either accepted by the buyer (a trade bill) or by a bank (a bank bill). The businessman selling the goods can thus turn the sale into cash very quickly by having the bill discounted, that is by selling it to a third party for cash for slightly less than its face value. The buyer of the goods benefits in that, depending on the payment date of the bill, he or she does not have to pay for the goods until they are delivered.

Bill finance, like other forms of short-term funds, may be useful when conditions for obtaining long-term funds tend to be difficult, but bills should not be heavily relied on for this purpose.

Export finance

For exports from the UK it is recognised that there may be a problem with cash collection, or at least prompt cash collection, in some countries. The Export Credits Guarantee Department provides assistance to exporters by:

(a) insuring exporters against the risk of non-payment; or
(b) providing unconditional guarantees of repayment to banks.

Similar facilities are now offered by some financial institutions in the private sector.

Medium-term finance

Finance that has a three- to ten-year repayment period is often called medium-term finance. It is obtainable in a number of forms, with varied uses and repayment patterns. The major uses of medium-term finance are as follows:

● to finance the purchase of assets with a corresponding life, such as plant and machinery;
● to replace a persistent overdraft;
● to provide the initial working capital requirements of the business.

Term loans

Bank loans are the most significant form of medium-term finance with fixed advances being made, usually on a secured basis. Loans are typically made to help firms acquire assets, and repayment is usually spread over the life of the asset, matching the income generated from the asset with the repayments of the loan.

European loans

Medium-term loans are available from certain institutions of the European Community, in particular the European Investment Bank (EIB) and the European Coal and Steel Community (ECSC).

The EIB makes loans to help finance industrial or infrastructure projects which aid regional development or are in the common interests of the European community. The loans, however, are limited to 50 per cent of the cost of the capital expenditure.

The ECSC makes loans for projects which generate new employment in areas affected by the run-down of the coal and steel industries. The loans are normally for eight years on terms broadly comparable with those offered by the EIB.

Loan Guarantee Scheme

If funds are not available through conventional sources, a firm may qualify for a loan under the government Small Firms Loan Guarantee Scheme. Under this scheme the government will guarantee 70 per cent (85 per cent in Inner City Task Force Areas in England) of the value of eligible term loans to small firms by the lenders (usually the clearing banks) participating in the scheme. Guarantees are available if the borrower is in an eligible business, the proposed business activity qualifies, and the loan itself is for an approved purpose. Eligible firms consist basically of small firms. The Department of Trade and Industry (DTI) will decide whether a firm is eligible in this respect. Most sectors of the economy involving tradeable goods and services are regarded as qualifying activities.

The DTI will charge a premium for its guarantee, at the rate of 2.5 per cent of the guaranteed amount (ie 70/85 per cent) of the total loan. This adds 1.75 per cent (2.12 per cent on guarantees of 85 per cent) per annum to the cost of borrowing. The premium will reduce as the loan is repaid. The premium is payable quarterly in advance.

Loans may be from two to seven years with the possibility of a capital repayment holiday of up to two years. The maximum which may be borrowed under the scheme is £100,000.

Long-term finance

Long-term finance normally refers to equity finance and sums borrowed for periods exceeding ten years. The major uses of long-term finance are as follows:

- to fund the acquisition of fixed assets with a long working life such as the purchase or construction of buildings;
- to provide semi-permanent working capital;
- to finance corporate acquisitions.

Equity and venture capital

Most businesses begin with an individual or individuals providing the initial equity capital from their own resources. A potential investor will expect the proprietor to inject sufficient equity to provide a basis for a viable business, and to indicate his or her commitment to that business. This often involves raising personal finance by pledging existing assets as security (eg a second mortgage on the proprietor's home).

However, apart from this source, a number of venture capital and other investment institutions specialise in the provision of start-up capital. Established public companies, too, may provide part of the capital needed to start a business if it is going to produce a product or service that will be useful to them.

Equity investment has been given an incentive by the government's Business Expansion Scheme. This scheme was introduced to encourage investment in the equity capital of unquoted companies; these investments carry risks, but also the chance of considerable rewards. The Business Expansion Scheme provides a generous tax incentive to the investor which can substantially reduce the cost of the investment and therefore increase the potential return on it. The investor gets relief at his or her highest marginal rate of tax (up to 40 per cent) so long as he or she is purchasing newly issued ordinary shares in an unquoted company.

To be eligible for BES investment, the unquoted company must have a qualifying trade. There are specific exceptions which include: dealing in land, shares or commodities, leasing and letting assets on hire, and banking, insurance and other financial services.

Long-term borrowings
Since commercial lenders will often restrict the granting of term loans for periods in excess of ten years to borrowers with proven track records and sound future prospects, we will confine our attention here to mortgage loans.

Mortgage loans are used for the purchase of specific assets such as land and buildings, the assets themselves being pledged as security to the lender. Such loans can extend to up to 35 years and while most institutional lenders prefer a lower limit of some £50,000, special mortgage schemes for as little as £5000 can be found.

Public sector finance

In addition to the foregoing types of finance, a wide range of central and local government incentives is available to companies of all sizes. The following are the main types of assistance:

National investment support
The government gives financial support for investment throughout the UK in a variety of ways. These include grants to study and implement new technology projects, grants to ease the cost of introducing quality assurance procedures, capital and industrial building allowances, and the provision of guarantees to commercial lenders under the Loan Guarantee Scheme.

Regional investment support

As part of its package of investment support, particular emphasis is given to the development and expansion of businesses in areas of high unemployment and industrial decline. These are the 'assisted areas', and assistance can take the form of regional development grants, regional selective assistance, in-plant training schemes and regional loans from the European Community.

Training and labour redevelopment support

The Department of Employment (DoE) and the Training Agency (previously the Manpower Services Commission) provide a range of schemes and services for the training and redevelopment of labour, and the development of work opportunities and experience for school-leavers and the long-term unemployed.

Small firms support

The Department of Employment's Small Firms Division co-ordinates and implements policy towards small firms. A wide range of information to assist small businesses is published by the Department.

Inner urban area support

These areas can often present special problems, and the government has therefore established a number of areas where industrial activity is encouraged by the offering of tax and loan incentives and the reduction or simplification of reporting and administrative requirements.

Other support

The support given by national and local government is extremely varied in range and depth and often depends on the location of the business. For example, there are grants available in South Wales to encourage the growth of local businesses, which would not be available in the South East of England. It is essential in setting up a business to talk to the government agencies about what may be available.

Sources of finance

The sources of finance generally available are summarised below:

Short-term finance

- Clearing banks
- Merchant banks

- Other British and foreign banks
- Finance houses
- Discount houses
- Factoring companies
- Leasing companies.

Medium-term finance

- Clearing banks
- Merchant banks
- Other British and foreign banks
- Finance houses
- Leasing companies
- Venture capital and other specialist investment institutions
- Public sector agencies.

Long-term finance

- Clearing banks
- Merchant banks
- Insurance companies
- Pension funds
- Venture capital and other specialist investment institutions
- Other British and foreign banks
- Public sector agencies.

Equity capital

- Venture capital and other specialist investment institutions
- Investment trust companies
- Pension funds
- Insurance companies
- Public sector agencies
- Merchant banks.

Negotiating the finance

Presenting a case for finance to an outside party can be thought of in terms of a number of distinct stages; each step must be passed before the financing proposal can proceed to the next stage. The approach adopted by a venture capitalist (providing equity finance) is different from that used by a clearing bank (providing overdraft and term loans). However, both providers will base their decisions on a good business plan well presented by competent management. Ultimately they will ask themselves if the business is viable or not!

Venture capital

A business plan and other relevant documentation must be sent to the lender or investor in advance of a meeting. As this is a very impressionable stage, it is recommended that such documents are neat and comprehensive.

The second stage is to attend a preliminary meeting with the prospective financier. This is a crucial stage as here the lender/investor will be able to assess the commitment, enthusiasm and business acumen of the individual or individuals presenting the case.

If the lender/investor gains a favourable impression of the sponsors, he or she will then go on to evaluate the purpose and terms of the business's financing requirements. If the proposal is deemed to be too risky relative to the return on the investor's money, the scheme will be rejected.

The next phase is likely to involve another round of interviews, to evaluate further the prospects of the business. Specifically, such factors as the unique aspects of the business, the likely future environment in which the company will be operating and the strengths and weaknesses of the business will be measured against the investor's or lender's own in-house lending criteria.

The investor/lender, if satisfied with the result of these interviews, will then proceed to have the company's projections closely scrutinised. This will include deriving some important ratios such as the gearing levels, the potential for liquidity, solvency, profitability and balance sheet strength.

At this stage, the sponsors will appreciate how they and their business ideas are perceived by the potential investor, and how risky the venture is considered to be by the investor/lender in terms of:

- the size of the expected return;
- when the return will materialise;
- how certain the return is; and
- how secure the basic investment/loan is.

It is at this point that the proprietor has to consider how much equity the venture capitalist may require in return for his or her investment, and proceed not to give away any more than is necessary in the ensuing negotiations.

Equity backers want only a minority stake in a company; they do not want to end up controlling or owning the business. They usually want capital growth rather than a regular flow of dividend income, and they certainly want the probability of an exit; in other words the prospect of being able to sell their shares either on a quoted market or in some other way some years ahead. Different equity investors have different expectations with regard to their management involvement in the business. Those seeking an active role will probably be less demanding in the negotiating procedure than those who wish to take a more passive role, in the belief that the company will be able to make good its promises.

Many proprietors are concerned at giving up equity in their business but it is better to own 80 per cent of a company which has the potential to grow than 100 per cent of a stagnant business.

Clearing banks

Most entrepreneurs see the clearing bank as the first port of call when establishing a business or looking for funds for expansion. The banks recognise that there is a growing need for them to provide not only finance which is extensive both in range and type but also sound commercial advice to their customers. Hence, in recent years, the clearing banks have established centres (either branches or distinct units) where corporate expertise can be concentrated to the benefit of the customer.

Many people approach a bank manager on the basis that the money is there for the asking. However, it is important to realise that the manager is acting as a trustee for the bank's shareholders and depositors. The banker will want to know when he will get his money back and that during the period of the loan he can earn his predetermined return (interest). Thus, his prime consideration is the cash flow; that is, will the business generate sufficient cash to meet its debts as and when they fall due, pay the interest on the borrowings and meet loan repayments, again as and when they fall due?

By and large the clearing banks are not in the risk business and the manager will be looking for adequate security to support the bank lending.

The main information required by the bank manager will be your business plan which should be sent in advance of any meeting. At the meeting the manager will appraise the management of the business and its ability to implement the plans as presented.

The level of finance required will very much determine whether or not the bank manager is able to give you a decision at that meeting. Each manager has a predetermined lending level above which it is necessary to refer the proposal to more senior personnel in the bank. It may therefore be necessary to attend further meetings or provide additional information before a decision is made.

The bank will be looking for security to cover its lending to the business. With reference to the proprietor it may require a personal guarantee and/or a charge over personal assets (such as the home). The bank may also require a charge over the company's assets which will give it priority over other creditors if the business should fail. It is essential to take professional advice before completing any legal documentation required by the bank.

To summarise: the raising of finance can be long and frustrating. Good preparation and a sound business plan will greatly enhance your ability to attract funds. If you are turned down by one source of finance, do not give up as your proposal may appeal to and fit the criteria of another lender.

4
Structuring the Business

Before you start trading, you must decide what legal form your business will take as this affects taxation and the accounting records you are required to keep. The four main forms of business organisation in the United Kingdom and their principal characteristics are as follows:

Sole trader

- You are the sole owner of the business.
- You are personally liable for all business debts.
- You can start trading whenever you like.
- No statutory requirements govern the format of the accounting records.
- There is no need to have annual accounts audited.
- There are no legal formalities to complete before commencing to trade.
- You may be required to register for Value Added Tax (VAT) and Pay As You Earn (PAYE) purposes and maintain records sufficient to make the necessary returns.

Partnerships

- You own the business jointly with one or more people.
- Each partner is personally liable for all the firm's business debts.
- A partnership, like a sole trader, has the advantage of secrecy in that it is not obliged to publish its accounts or have them audited.
- Similar requirements to a sole trader with reference to VAT and PAYE.
- A partnership may be created without any legal formalities, as the provisions of the Partnership Act 1890 will be taken as the

partnership agreement. However, it is usual to draw up an agreement at the start of trading; otherwise a successful working arrangement may be spoilt by disagreement over such basic issues as:
- profit-sharing arrangements;
- partners' drawings;
- capital contributions;
- voting rights;
- admitting or expelling a partner;
- withdrawal from the partnership.

Limited company

- The most common form of business entity.
- A limited company (incorporated under the Companies Act 1985) is a separate legal entity from the shareholders and directors. It may contract, sue and be sued in its own name and capacity.
- The shareholders are not liable for the company's debts beyond the amount remaining unpaid on the shares or beyond any amount guaranteed to a third party (such as a bank).
- Incorporation also involves the preparation of accounts for the company, and having these and the accounting records audited. This must be carried out once a year by a firm of qualified accountants.
- A limited company must, each year, file with the Registrar of Companies a set of audited accounts, which include a directors' report, auditors' report, profit and loss account, balance sheet, source and application of funds and explanatory notes to the figures in the accounts. In addition it is necessary to file an annual return (cost £20) giving details of the directors, shareholders and certain other statutory information. All information on file at the Companies' Registry is open to inspection by the public.
- Registration of a limited company involves the filing of certain documents with the Registrar of Companies. While this is not unduly complicated, it is not a matter to be undertaken lightly and involves a number of pitfalls. Professional advice should be sought. It is important to remember that the various documents, including the Memorandum and Articles of Association which give details of the company's constitution, its legal form, its business and its powers, have to be lodged with the Registrar of Companies before a company exists and can begin to trade.

Throughout the rest of this book the word 'company' refers to a limited liability company.

Unlimited company

A less common but sometimes useful entity is the unlimited company which combines characteristics of both incorporated and unincorporated bodies in that, for taxation purposes, it is treated as a company, but the liability of the shareholders is unlimited as far as all creditors of the company are concerned.

There are certain businesses, regulated by professional bodies, which are required to trade as unlimited entities and, in some cases, an unlimited company is preferable to a partnership or sole proprietorship.

It is not unusual for a business to commence as a sole trader, become a partnership and ultimately incorporate as it grows.

Advantages and disadvantages

The decision as to which legal entity is appropriate to your particular circumstances is a complex matter and various advantages and disadvantages are listed below. In summary you should consider the following:

Sole trader/Partnership

Advantages
- Easy to start up.
- No legal formalities but partnerships should always have a partnership deed.
- Relative freedom from legislative control. No requirement to file audited accounts or information on public record concerning the business. Only accounts for VAT and PAYE required plus Inland Revenue tax return.
- No requirement to have an auditor.
- Taxed as self-employed which can have tax advantages in the first three years of trading.
- After three years, tax paid in arrears on previous year's profit.
- Advantageous rules on losses.
- Low National Insurance contributions. Self-employed pay Class 2 and Class 4 contributions:
  Class 2 – £4.25 per week
  Class 4 – 6.30 per cent on profits between £5,050 and £16,900 (maximum; 1989/90 figures).
- More favourable tax treatment of deductible expenses for tax purposes. 'Wholly and exclusively ... for the purposes of the business' as opposed to 'Wholly, exclusively and necessarily in the

performance of duties' for company expenses.
- Retirement relief provisions are more flexible than those which apply to shareholdings in limited companies.
- Financial flexibility with regard to sharing profits.

Disadvantages
- Some suppliers will not deal with sole traders and partnerships due to lack of statutory and 'financial control'.
- Unlimited liability. Unless there is a limited partnership an individual is liable for all losses of business; partners are jointly and severally liable.
- An individual could lose all his or her assets and therefore face bankruptcy.
- 'Closing' year's tax treatment when the business ceases – timing important.
- Profit taxed at personal rates, top rate being 40 per cent.
- Need to make independent pension provision – less advantageous rules than for companies.
- Tax problems can arise on incorporating at a later stage.
- Raising finance can be difficult.
- Partnership can be difficult to run – direction a problem.
- No statutory protection of business name.

Limited company

Advantages
- Limited liability. Shareholders' liability limited to amount of share capital contributed.
- Favoured trading medium by suppliers as tightly controlled by statute.
- Directors not liable if they 'follow the rules'.
- Easier to introduce new business partners.
- Ideal vehicle for expansion (Stock Exchange quotations).
- Can give fixed and floating charges on company assets.
- Easier to pass the company down from generation to generation.
- Some business sectors require the 'kudos' of limited liability.
- Continuity of existence.
- Protection of company names.
- Tax efficient ways of getting shares into the hands of employees through employee share schemes.
- Business Expansion Scheme relief available for investors in qualifying companies.

- Company pension scheme can provide greater benefits than self-employed arrangements.

Disadvantages
- Limited liability could be negated in practice by director/shareholders having to give personal guarantees to third parties.
- Disclosure of information (for example, about the company through filing audited accounts, annual returns, Memorandum and Articles of Association).
- Tightly regulated through provisions in the Companies Act 1985, Insolvency Act 1986, Company Directors' Disqualification Act 1986.
- Heavy penalties under statute if rules 'not followed'. Also personal financial liability may be incurred.
- High set-up costs and annual running costs.
- High National Insurance contributions:
  Employer maximum 10.45 per cent
  Employee maximum 9 per cent.
- Directors paid under PAYE.
- Less beneficial treatment of deductible expenses and 'benefits in kind'.
- Less flexible profit-sharing arrangements.
- Statutory records to be kept.
- Stamp duty to pay on transfers of shares.
- Restriction on loans to directors.
- Double charge to capital gains tax
  - first charge on the company or gains made by selling its assets.
  - second charge on the shareholders realising their shares in the company.
- Directors cannot use business funds for personal use without an assessment to income tax as a benefit in kind arising.
- Two shareholders required – otherwise sole member is personally liable.

Other factors linked to incorporation

Commercial considerations

Market-place image can be extremely important when starting a business because customers and suppliers must be inspired to trade with you confidently, and that means giving the impression that the organisation is well run and soundly based. For many people this is best suggested by adopting limited company status.

**Inland Revenue
Corporation Tax**

The Secretary

Dear Sir/Madam,

I shall be grateful if you will supply the information requested overleaf and at the same time **forward a copy of the Company's Memorandum and Articles of Association for me to retain.**

May I remind you that-

- the company should

    - operate Pay As You Earn in respect of all remuneration paid (including fees, etc., paid or credited to directors)

    - deduct National Insurance Contributions

- the company is required to make returns to the Collector of Taxes

    - of all qualifying distributions and the Advance Corporation Tax payable in respect of them,

    - of certain amounts of Franked Investment Income received, and

    - of all annual payments etc. and the income tax deducted from them.

You may like to keep the attached copy as a record of your reply.

Yours faithfully,

District date stamp

H.M Inspector of Taxes

CT41G

**Inland Revenue
Income Tax**

Reference

Dear Sir/Madam

I understand that you are now in business on your own account or subcontracting in the Construction Industry and I shall be obliged if you will let me have the information asked for below and overleaf as soon as possible.

If this is the first time you have been in business on your own account a booklet IR28 entitled "Starting in Business" is available on request to help explain your tax position. If there are any further income tax points on which you are in doubt you may like to call here. If so, I shall be pleased to arrange an appointment.

National Insurance Contributions (Class 2) are normally payable when you become self employed and you should contact your local DHSS Office about this.

Yours faithfully,

District date stamp

H.M. Inspector of Taxes

Enquiries about yourself and any business partners

Yourself

Your surname	Tax Office to which last Income Tax Return made *
Your first names	
Your private address	Reference in that Office *
	National Insurance Number
Postcode	
	Date of birth

* If you are a married woman the answers to these questions should relate to the husband.

Business partners

	Partner 1	Partner 2	Partner 3
Partner's surname			
Partner's first names			
Partner's private address			
	Postcode	Postcode	Postcode

If you have more than three business partners please give the names and addresses of any other partners on a separate sheet

41G(1987)

**Inland Revenue
PAYE**

Reference

District date stamp

Details of Directors

Please let me have the details asked for below. This will help me to give the directors the correct code numbers.

If the directors can tell you their last Tax Offices and reference numbers it may avoid separate enquiries to each director.

Surname, first name(s) and private address	National Insurance number	Last known Tax Office and reference
Postcode		
Postcode		
Postcode		
Postcode		
Postcode		

District date stamp

P222

3766/0307L Dd 8993308 75M 5/87 TP Gp607

**Inland Revenue
PAYE**

The PAYE way of deducting tax from pay applies to any employee or director you pay

- at a rate of more than £   a week or £   a month
- at a rate of more than £1 a week or £4 a month and who have not certified on P46 that this is the only or main employment.

National Insurance contributions apply to any employee or director you pay

- £   or more in any week or £   or more in a month.

If you are already operating PAYE or taking off National Insurance contributions or making deductions under the Subcontractors Deduction Scheme please show your Tax District and full PAYE reference and send the form back to me. You do not need to answer the questions over the page.

District name

Reference number

/

If you have no directors or employees within the scope of PAYE or National Insurance contributions please send this form back to me and write 'NONE' in this box.

If you have any employee or director within the scope of PAYE or National Insurance contributions but you are **not** operating PAYE please answer the questions over the page and send the form back to me. I will let you have details of how to work out PAYE and NIC.

If any employee or director has handed you a "leaving certificate" (form P45 parts 2 and 3) from a previous employer, and you have not already sent the completed part 3 to this office please complete and enclose it with this form.

District date stamp

P223

5560-0765L Dd 8096317 150M 5/88 TP Gp607

BEFORE COMPLETING THIS AUTHORITY YOU ARE
ADVISED TO READ THE NOTES OVERLEAF

To: H.M. Inspector of Taxes .... **District**

Inspector's reference ....

Name of person to be assessed ....

NOTICES OF ASSESSMENT

Until further notice, please send copies of any notices of assessment to income tax, Class 4 NIC, corporation tax and
capital gains tax, including any explanatory forms required to accompany such notices, to—

Agent's name ....

    Address ....
    (including
    postcode) ....

    ....

    Reference ....

    { I have previously authorised my agent to receive copy notices under the arrangement which existed before
        6 April 1974.

        This authority is for the purpose of including notices of assessment to ....

*{

    ....

                  (enter tax and, if income tax, a description of the income)

    at...District under reference ....

I hereby withdraw any earlier request that copies of notices of assessment should be sent to any other agent.

*I wish this authority to be applied to all my income or gains currently subject to assessment.

Signature .... Date .... 19 ....

**Complete or delete as appropriate*

FOR OFFICIAL USE		Initials	Date
	Sch. D/"taxed" income working sheet(s) noted		
	Concard/HR-S Regr./Centre record noted		
	133U/133U-1/133P-1 or CT 133 noted		
	Form(s) 64-6 issued		
	Form CZ1 or CZ4 issued *(companies only)*		

64–8 (New)

Dd 8263831 600M 12/82 Edl 204851)

Like other images, this one is exaggerated; incorporation cannot ensure reliability or respectability. However, by becoming a company you show that you are willing to work within the controls and requirements of the Companies Act 1985.

Tax considerations
Commercial considerations should always outweigh tax considerations. However, if commercial considerations make little or no difference to the best form of business to adopt, consideration of the tax implications may help you to reach a decision.

A company is required to pay corporation tax and a sole trader or partnership income tax on profits earned. It is necessary to inform your local Inspector of Taxes of your existence and the following forms should be completed as appropriate:

CT41G   Inland Revenue Corporation Tax (for companies).
41G(1987)   Inland Revenue Income Tax (for sole traders and
               partnerships).
P222   PAYE: Particulars of Directors (for companies).
P223(1987)   Inland Revenue PAYE.
64–8 (New)   Notices of Assessment (authorising the Inland
               Revenue to send copies of the assessments to your pro-
               fessional advisers).

These forms are reproduced on pages 37–41.

Sole traders/Partnerships
Sole traders and partnerships are charged income tax at the rate applicable during the fiscal year (6 April to 5 April). The rates are as follows:

	1987/88 Taxable income £	Rate	1988/89 Taxable income £	Rate	1989/90 Taxable income £	Rate
First	17,900	27%	19,300	25%	20,700	25%
Next	2,500	40%				
Next	5,000	45%				
Next	7,900	50%				
Next	7,900	55%				
	Remainder	60%	Remainder	40%	Remainder	40%

There may also be a liability to Class 2 and Class 4 National Insurance contributions depending on the level of profit in each fiscal year. Class 2 contributions are at a weekly stamp rate of £4.25. Class 4 contributions are levied at 6.3 per cent on profits between £5050 and £16,900 (maximum). Income tax and Class 4 National Insurance contributions are due in two instalments on 1 January and 1 July.

Companies

Companies are charged corporation tax at the rate applicable during the financial year, which for tax purposes runs from 1 April to 31 March. Where a company's year end is not 31 March, the profits for the year are apportioned and the appropriate rate charged.

The corporation tax rates applicable for the years 1986–1990 are:

	Small companies' profits below £100,000/£150,000	Normal rate profits over £500,000/£750,000
31 March 1986	30%	40%
31 March 1987	29%	35%
31 March 1988	27%	35%
31 March 1989	25%	35%
31 March 1990	25%	35%

The rates for profits falling between £100,000 and £500,000 (up to 31 March 1989) and £150,000 and £750,000 (31 March 1990) are such as to ensure that the tax charge rises progressively and that the overall tax paid is between the small and normal company rate.

Corporation tax is generally due nine months after the company's year end.

Remuneration

Sole traders/Partnerships

In this situation the owner of the business or the partner is treated as a self-employed individual. Drawings can be made from the business during the course of the year without paying tax, but the owner is liable to pay tax on all profits whether drawn out of the business or not.

Shareholders/Proprietors

In a limited company the shareholders may also be directors of the company. For tax purposes they are treated as employees of the company and all remuneration paid to them must be subject to tax under the PAYE system.

Personal considerations

The degree of risk which an individual runs depends partly on the form of business structure adopted. Theoretically, a sole trader takes the greater risk in that he or she must meet the liabilities of the business out of his or her own funds if necessary. The members of a partnership are in a similar position, although they may have a wider asset base. Shareholders in a limited company know that the most they can lose is the money they paid for their shares, unless personal guarantees have been made to a bank or another third party.

Each person's attitude to risk depends upon personal opinions and circumstances. There are many other factors which can only be weighed by the individual, such as the following:

- Do I have sufficient business acumen to run a business by myself, or would it be wiser to collaborate with other people who have complementary skills?
- Am I prepared to have the operation of the business governed by the restrictions of company law?
- Am I prepared to pay incorporation and audit costs?
- Do I have long-term plans for the business and the financing of it, or do I envisage a short-term venture to take advantage of temporary market opportunities?
- A further consideration now stems from the provisions of the Insolvency Act 1986 in respect of the disqualification and personal liability of directors, and the next section is devoted to the responsibilities of directors in general and to their potential liabilities in particular.

Duties of directors

Anyone who sets out in business and forms a company will find him or herself having to take on the role and responsibilities of a director. This role may be described as the overall direction, management and operation of the company.

To satisfy the law, a private company must have at least one director. There must also be a company secretary, and a sole director cannot also be the company secretary.

The first directors of a company are usually appointed by the subscribers to the company's Memorandum and Articles of Association, the documents which give details of the company's constitution, legal form, its business and its powers.

Thereafter, the directors normally have the power, at any time, to appoint a person to fill a vacancy caused by the sudden departure of a director from the board, or to appoint an additional director. A company may remove a director and appoint another person in his or her place.

The company's Articles of Association may disqualify a director from acting as such in certain circumstances, or may require that his or her office be vacated. Such circumstances include:

- if a director becomes bankrupt or of unsound mind;
- if he or she is convicted of an offence in connection with the promotion, formation or management of the company, or of any fraud;
- if, by notice in writing, he or she resigns the office of director; or
- if he or she is absent from board meetings for more than six months without the other directors' permission.

Conduct of directors

The general principles of current law governing the accountability of directors may be dealt with under two headings: good faith, and skill and care.

Good faith

A director must observe the utmost good faith towards the company in any transaction with it or on its behalf. As an agent and officer of the company, the director must exercise the powers vested in him or her in the interests of the company as a whole, having regard to the interests of the company's employees as well as those of its shareholders. Since the director is in a position of trust, he or she must disregard private interests where there might be a conflict.

The director must act honestly and with diligence in exercising the powers of office, and where any power is exercised it must be for the purpose for which it was intended. A director may not, therefore, make a personal profit from information or opportunities arising from his or her position as director; any such profit must be accounted for to the company.

Skill and care

In the case of an executive director, usually appointed for some expertise, and under a contract of service, it is implied in such a contract that the person will exercise reasonable skill and care which can be expected of someone in his or her position.

In the case of a non-executive director without relevant qualifications or experience in business, the skill and care expected is subjective; that is, the director must do his or her best.

For a director having particular qualifications and/or experience in business the standard is objective: he or she is bound to exercise such skill and care as may be expected from a person of such professional skill or experience.

Under the Insolvency Act 1986, a court can disqualify a director from office for a minimum period of two years where he or she is or has been a director of a company that has become insolvent, and where his or her conduct as a director of that company makes him or her unfit to be involved in the management of any company. The Act applies equally if the director has been incompetent or dishonest. Moreover, the provisions apply where a company has gone into insolvent liquidation and he or she was a director of the company in the 24 months preceding the liquidation, as there is an assumed duty to persuade colleagues on the board of the error of their ways, and to insist that they take competent and timely advice.

In addition, if, at some time before the winding-up of a company, a director knew or ought to have concluded that there was no reasonable prospect of that company avoiding insolvent liquidation, a court, on application by the liquidator, may ask the director to contribute to that company's assets as the court thinks proper.

Thus, the Insolvency Act has introduced new responsibilities which any individual considering incorporation would be foolish to overlook.

Co-operatives

Another possibility in starting a business would be to form a co-operative with your fellow workers. In such an organisation the running of the business is controlled by its workforce, ie they make the decisions on who should manage the business, safeguard assets and what its aims are to be.

It is still necessary to establish a legal entity. This can take the form of a partnership, limited company or registration as a co-operative society.

Franchising

A franchise system operates on the basis that an entrepreneur (known as the franchisor) will have developed a particular business (eg a print shop providing photocopying facilities, printing, stationery etc, or a hamburger restaurant) and wishes to expand into other locations by granting a franchise to another party (the franchisee) to operate a similar business. The franchisor will make sure that the franchisee is a suitable person to run the business, and it is equally important for the franchisee to make full and careful investigation of how successful the particular franchise is and to talk to existing franchisees. Once the parties agree, the franchisee will normally make an initial payment to the franchisor and in return will receive help and advice in setting up the business. The franchisee will have to deal with all the matters in relation to raising finance, preparing a business plan and establishing a legal entity as mentioned before. The franchisee will continue to make payments to the franchisor, usually based on levels of turnover or profit.

The main advantages of a franchise are that a lot of the initial problems of setting up a business will be relieved by the help and experience of the franchisor and that you are working with an established business. The element of risk in setting up your business is therefore reduced.

The main disadvantage is that while it is your own business, there will be a significant level of control by, and you will be paying a proportion of your income to, the franchisor. You may wish to take greater risks in establishing your own business in the hope of higher rewards.

Before entering into any franchising agreement it is essential that you obtain professional advice from your accountant or solicitor.

5
Setting Up the Business

Introduction

This chapter covers in detail the various matters which will need consideration, and in many instances action, before your trading entity can make the first product, sell the first item or supply the first service.

These matters are as follows:

- bank accounts must be opened;
- trading premises must be found;
- trading terms must be set;
- relevant authorities must be informed;
- if employees are recruited, a PAYE scheme must be set up;
- application for VAT registration must be made;
- letterheads, invoices and stationery must be printed, and nameplates obtained; and
- insurance cover must be obtained.

Bank accounts and cheque signatories

Before trading commences, it will be necessary to open a current account with a bank, and possibly also a deposit account. The bank will require completion of a mandate and copies of the Articles of Association and Certificate of Incorporation in the case of a company.

In doing this you will need to decide who the cheque signatories will be, and determine their level of authority. The bank should then be informed of these details in writing, and given instructions as to the provision of pre-printed cheque books and paying-in books, how frequently you will require bank statements – at least monthly, but possibly more often than that – and details of standing orders, direct debits and credit transfers required.

Very frequently, at the start-up of a new business, overdraft and/or loan facilities are required and you will have prepared a business plan as described in Chapter 2. In the case of an unincorporated business, the bank may demand that their loan or overdraft is secured on property belonging to the proprietor, which may or may not be part of the assets of the business. In the case of companies, banks frequently require personal guarantees from the directors and a charge over the company's assets (known as a debenture). Professional advice should be sought from your accountant or solicitor before completing the documentation required by the bank.

The bank will also wish to know how your business is progressing and to make comparisons against your original budgets and cash flows. You will need to agree the frequency with which you supply the bank manager with copies of your management accounts and other information as described in Chapter 8.

Where are you going to trade from?

The acquisition of property is a complex process and you need to give yourself plenty of time and plan well in advance of commencing business. Many businesses commence trading from home and, while this will achieve cost savings initially, it is likely that you will quickly outgrow the space available. Professional advice is essential but before taking such advice you should consider the following:

Initial considerations

- The type of building may be important. Many older buildings have awkward shapes which may not be suitable to your business and cause inefficiencies. A small light industrial unit or a new warehouse may be more suitable and give you the scope to design the interior to your particular needs.
- Check that the building can be used for both office and factory purposes. Many buildings, particularly older ones, are used for purposes not permitted by the local authority.
- The building should be large enough for your present and anticipated near future requirements.
- Ensure that the utilities (gas, electricity etc) you require are available and in sufficient quantity for your needs.
- Consider parking and loading areas around your premises.
- What are the security arrangements for the site? Will you have to install a sophisticated security system yourself?

- What other items are there specific to your particular business (waste disposal, ventilation etc)?

Where do you want to be?
The location of your premises will often be essential to the success of your business and you need to think about the following questions:

- Should it be a retail location?
- What are the local transport facilities and proximity to trunk routes?
- How close are you to suppliers/customers?
- Are the skills that you need available in the area?
- Are there any town planning requirements/restrictions?
- Where is your competition?
- What grants are available?
- Any personal reason (where you live, family commitments, schools etc)?

What sort of premises do you need?
The following matters should be considered:

- The amount of space required (splitting between office, factory, warehouse).
- The type of building – is a prominent or prestigious building necessary (and can you afford it)?

What type of building do you require?
There are both advantages and disadvantages in new and existing buildings, some of which are set out below for consideration:

- A new building will have lower repair and maintenance costs, at least for the first five to ten years.
- A new building will have better thermal insulation, thus reducing heating bills, and will have been designed to comply with current health and safety and fire regulations, which may be expensive to update in an older building.
- A new building can be designed to your own requirements, and to allow for future expansion, but it may be difficult and expensive to make alterations to an existing building.
- A new building may look cleaner and more impressive and this may be important if you expect your customers to come to you.
- There is more choice of older buildings available on the market at any time, and you will probably be able to move in more quickly than if a building is designed and built to your specific requirements.

- An existing building will probably be cheaper to rent or buy.
- An older building will not hold its value as an investment as well as a new building, particularly if the location is poor.
- While it may be cheaper to acquire or lease an older property the cost of conversion may ultimately mean higher costs than acquiring a purpose-built factory. It is essential that you list the pros and cons and determine which is the most cost efficient in the long term.

Are you going to buy or lease?

You will need to consider whether you will purchase the property outright from the previous owner (freehold) or lease over a period of time from the owner (leasehold).

In general terms, freehold is preferable to leasehold property as you will have the benefit of capital appreciation and, as long as you remain within the law, be able to do what you like with it. If you outgrow your premises, it should be easier to dispose of a freehold rather than a leasehold property.

However, on a practical note, most new businesses cannot afford to purchase a building outright and find both interest and capital repayments on the funds borrowed to buy the property. Therefore, the first major commitment of a company is often the acquisition of leasehold premises.

Leases are invariably lengthy and complex legal documents requiring the expert consideration of your solicitor. When considering a lease you need to bear in mind the following:

- If the lease is a new one, the company will remain responsible for it for its entire duration, even if management later assign or sublet the property. Landlords can bring actions for recovery of outstanding rents unpaid by the present tenant against the previous tenants unless the previous tenant was specifically released from all covenants under the lease.
- The landlord may require personal guarantees from the directors of a company.
- You may wish to assign the lease or sublet the premises. Are there any restrictions in the lease?
- What is the period of the rent review (normally, three, five or seven years)?
- If you carry out improvements to the premises, will these be reflected in your next rent review?
- What is the length of the lease and any break points (options to terminate by one party or the other)?
- Are there any restrictions on the use of the premises?
- What is your liability to dilapidations?

Who can you go to for help?

Professionals: chartered surveyors and estate agents

Advice should be sought from friends and colleagues with a personal knowledge of the professional firms in your area before you select one to find a property for you. You should agree terms in advance, and brief the agent in detail as to your requirements and price range. He or she will then negotiate the best deal possible on your behalf. These professional firms are also particularly qualified to act for you in planning matters, and in valuations if required for a mortgage application.

Local and national newspapers

Studying the industrial and commercial property advertisements in the press will give you a good idea of availability and price.

Government agencies

The Department of Trade and Industry (DTI) has a great deal of information available on Enterprise Zones, special development and development areas, and details of assistance (mostly financial) to encourage businesses to locate in these areas. The Small Firms Service will be able to advise on which of the various agencies will be most suitable to help you.

Some local authorities are particularly keen to encourage new businesses to start up in their areas, and have grants available to help, so the local Enterprise Agency or industrial promotional unit should be contacted.

Have you thought of the other costs?

Your budget should also include the add-on costs of acquiring premises:

- Removals to the premises if applicable.
- Fitting out the various areas for the purposes for which they will be used, and arranging for gas, electricity and water to be laid on. You may also need to arrange for refuse collection and purchase the appropriate containers.
- Furniture and equipment for the office which may include desks, chairs, filing cabinets, shelves, calculators, typewriters, word processors, a computer system, photocopiers, communications equipment ranging from telephone and telex to a facsimile machine and computer modems, vending machines and/or tea- and coffee-making facilities, perhaps a fridge, first aid equipment, fire extinguishers etc.

- Stationery will need to be printed ready for you to use as soon as you move to a new premises.
- Health and safety regulations. The rules and regulations are fairly complex. Advice on health and safety matters is given by Inspectors, and there is an extensive amount of technical material published by the Health and Safety Executive. A visit from the Health and Safety Officer can result in an unprepared company incurring additional expenditure.
- Fire regulations are strict and you should arrange for an inspection by a fire officer so that any costs of complying with the regulations can be allowed for in your budget.

Trading terms

Before you start you should set your terms of trade in relation to your sales. To a large extent these will probably be dictated by those of your competitors. Matters which you should consider are:

- responsibility for shipment and related costs;
- point at which title transfers to the buyer;
- insurance for goods in transit;
- terms of credit and discounts;
- method of payment;
- appointment of agents, if appropriate;
- period during which you will accept returned goods;
- period for which quotations will be held;
- arrangements for the cancellation of orders.

Before printing these, your solicitor should be asked to review your trading terms to ensure that they give you adequate protection and that they are legally enforceable.

Finally, these conditions must form part of the 'offer for sale' that you are making to your customers, and therefore it is essential that they are brought to the customers' attention. If they are printed on the back of quotations, order forms etc, attention should be drawn to them on the front of the form. They should also be on display at your premises, and printed in catalogues and price lists.

Pay As You Earn (PAYE)

Deduction of income tax and National Insurance contributions (NIC) under the PAYE system is obligatory for all organisations that have employees, including directors. Whether or not an individual is an employee in a particular situation is a question of fact depending on the terms under which he or she works. It is important for this to be clarified before an individual is taken on.

The following principal factors should be taken into account:

- the degree of control and supervision exercised over the individual's work;
- whether services are performed wholly or mainly for one business;
- where the duties are carried out;
- terms of pay, holiday time, pension arrangements and other benefits;
- whether the work has to be performed personally, or whether a substitute may be supplied;
- provision of own items of equipment;
- the financial risk and responsibility undertaken by the individual.

The Inland Revenue have issued leaflet IR56, entitled 'Tax: Employed or Self-employed' which sets out the guidelines of employment status; if doubt exists it should be clarified, and the Revenue have indicated that they expect to be consulted on difficult or uncertain cases. Obtaining prior Revenue agreement will avoid having to make a settlement later of liabilities to tax or National Insurance which the employer failed to deduct from the remuneration of a person who is held to be an employee rather than self-employed.

Having ascertained that you will need to operate PAYE, it is necessary to notify the Revenue office covering your geographical area. The telephone number of the nearest PAYE enquiry office can be found in the telephone directory, and from them the name of the Revenue office can be obtained.

The relevant forms which need to be submitted to the Inland Revenue were described in the previous chapter.

Upon registration, the Inland Revenue will send you:

- a PAYE reference number;
- Form P8 'How to operate the PAYE system' (introduction for employers on tax tables, completion of deductions working sheets, new and leaving employees etc);
- Employers' Guides to PAYE, National Insurance, Statutory Sick Pay (SSP) and Statutory Maternity Pay (SMP);
- supplies of the following forms:
    - P11 Deductions working sheet
    - P15 Coding claim form for completion by new employee
    - P45 Details of employee leaving.
    - P46 Notification to the Revenue where a new employee does not produce parts 2 and 3 of Form P45

P47   Application for authority to refund tax to new employee
in excess of £100

More information is given in Appendix 5.

In order to calculate the amount of tax and National Insurance payable by an employee, the Inland Revenue will supply you with sets of tables. By reference to 'Free Pay Tables' and an employee's tax code, you will be able to calculate the amount of salary which is not subject to tax at the end of the payment period. The difference between this and the gross salary is the employee's 'taxable pay'. The tax can then be calculated by reference to the 'Taxable Pay Tables'. The employer's and employee's National Insurance contributions are calculated by reference to the employee's gross pay in conjunction with the 'National Insurance Tables'.

Employers are also required to pay Statutory Sick Pay (SSP) to their employees who are off work for four or more days as a result of illness, accident or injury. The amount of SSP payable is laid down, and depends on the employee's average earnings for the preceding eight-week period. Total SSP payable (plus a percentage to compensate the employer for the employer's NIC) is deducted from the total National Insurance contributions payable to the Inland Revenue, so that in effect SSP is paid by the government. The 'Employer's Guide to Statutory Sick Pay' gives detailed guidance on the operation of SSP.

Statutory Maternity Pay (SMP) works like SSP in that it is paid to the employee in the same way that she would be paid her wages. SMP paid (plus compensation for employer's NIC) is then deducted from the National Insurance contributions payable to the Collector of Taxes. The 'Employer's Guide to Statutory Maternity Pay' sets out all the rules governing the administration of SMP.

The tax and National Insurance due (after deduction of any SSP and SMP paid) should be paid over to the Inland Revenue by the 19th of the month following that in which the salary is paid.

At the end of each year (5 April) the employer will be sent forms for completion summarising each employee's pay, deductions and SSP/SMP paid for the year (P14) and the employer's annual statement (P35), a summary form on which the employees are listed, with their total deductions and SSP/SMP for the year. These amounts are totalled and added to the amounts accounted for by the employer to the Inland Revenue.

In addition to deducting tax and National Insurance contributions during the year, an employer will have to complete returns at the end of the year which give details of expenses paid or reimbursed to employees during the year and also benefits provided.

Form P9D is used for employees earning less than £8500 per annum; Form P11D relates to employees earning more than this amount and all directors regardless of levels of remuneration.

In deciding whether the £8500 limit has been reached, it is necessary to include not only salary or wages but also the value of taxable benefits and reimbursed expenses before any claim is made for business use.

These forms will be issued to employers at the end of the tax year together with details regarding their completion. The forms are wide-ranging and employers should ensure that their records of employee expenses and benefits are sufficient to enable them to be completed. The non-completion or incorrect completion of these forms is an area which the Inland Revenue frequently investigate and which can lead to substantial tax liabilities.

Value Added Tax (VAT)

A trader is required to register for VAT purposes if either:

- annual taxable turnover is expected to exceed £23,600 per annum; or
- taxable turnover in the previous quarter exceeded £8000.

A 'taxable person' (a person or company who is registered or required to be registered under the VAT legislation) is required to account for VAT on supplies made (output tax) but is entitled to claim credit for VAT suffered or paid by him or her on goods or services supplied to him or her (input tax). If input tax exceeds output tax, a taxable person may claim a refund of the excess. Taxable persons therefore act as collecting agents for the tax. VAT is collected by HM Customs and Excise.

You can also apply for voluntary registration to reclaim net input tax. This can be beneficial in the early days of a business to enable you to reclaim VAT on the purchase of capital equipment and stock. Once registered for VAT a business will be expected to remain so for two years before de-registration can be considered.

Registration is obtained by completing Form VAT1 (reproduced on pp. 57–59) which can be obtained from your local VAT office (listed in the telephone directory) and returning it to them. They also have available numerous free publications explaining the VAT legislation and how it applies to different trades. In particular, the booklet 'Should I be registered for VAT?' will be of use to new businesses. There are various options available when determining how to account for the tax. It is advisable to consult your accountant as to the most appropriate method for your business.

VALUE ADDED TAX

Application for Registration

HM Customs and Excise

For official use

Date of receipt [_____] 1

Local office code and registration number

Name

Trade name

Taxable turnover

| | | | D | M | Y | | Stagger | Status |

Oversize name address | Computer user | Group Div. | | Intg. | | Overseas

Rept | Vol. | | | | | |

| | | | D | M | Y | |
Bn | | | | |

You should open up this form and read the notes before you answer these questions. Please write clearly in ink.

Applicant and business

1 Full name

2 Trading name

3 Address

Phone no.

Postcode

4 Status of business

Limited company [ ]   Company incorporation certificate no. [   ]   and date [day | month | year '19]

Sole proprietor [ ]   Partnership [ ]   Other-specify [   ]

5 Business activity [   ]   Trade classification [   ]

6 Computer user [ ]

Repayments of VAT

7 [ ]   Bank sorting code and account no. [   ]   National Girobank account no. [   ]

VAT 1

please continue overleaf ———▶

Compulsory registrations

8 Date of first taxable supply   day month year 19 | Value of taxable supplies in the 12 months from that date. £

9 Date from which you have to be registered   day month year 19

10 Exemption from compulsory registration

expected value of zero-rated supplies in the next 12 months   £

Other types of registration

11 Taxable supplies below registration limits ☐

value of taxable supplies in the last 12 months   £

12 No taxable supplies made yet ☐

(a) expected annual value of taxable supplies   £

(b) expected date of first taxable supply   day month year 19

Business changes and transfers

13 Business transferred as a going concern ☐

(a) date of transfer or change of legal status   day month year 19

(b) name of previous owner

(c) previous VAT registration number (if known)

14 Transfer of VAT registration number ☐

Related businesses

15 Other VAT registrations   Yes ☐   No ☐

Declaration – You must complete this declaration.

16 I _____

(Full name in BLOCK LETTERS)

declare that all the entered details and information in any accompanying documents are correct and complete.

Signature _____   Date _____

Proprietor ☐   Partner ☐   Director ☐   Company Secretary ☐   Authorised Official ☐   Trustee ☐

For official use

Registration	Obligatory	Exemption	Voluntary	Intending	Transfer of Regn. no.
Approved — Initial/Date					
Refused — Initial/Date					
Form Issued — Initial/Date	VAT 9/Other	VAT 8	VAT 7	Letter	Approval Letter

VAT 1 F3733(APRIL 1986)

Compulsory registrations

8 Give the date on which you made your first taxable supply of goods or services to a customer. Then give the total value of taxable supplies that you have made, or expect to make, in the 12 months from that date.

If your taxable supplies are below the compulsory registration limits, leave these boxes blank and go on to Question 11. If you have not made a taxable supply, leave these boxes blank and go on to Question 12.

You will find more about taxable supplies in paragraphs 2 and 3 of the registration booklet. Normally the value of your taxable supplies will be your total turnover. If you are unsure about whether or not to include some items – such as donations or grants – please check with your local VAT office.

9 **You must answer this question even if you are applying for exemption under Question 10.**

You should read paragraph 6 of the registration booklet before you answer this question. If you decide that you have to register, you must give the date from which you have to be registered. If you wish to register from a date earlier than you have to, please enclose a letter explaining why and from what date.

10 You can apply for exemption from registration if you would not normally be liable to pay VAT to Customs and Excise because your taxable supplies are wholly or mainly zero-rated. If you want to apply for exemption from registration, you should:

- tick the box; **and**
- give the value of the zero-rated supplies you expect to make in the next 12 months.

Paragraph 7 of the registration booklet tells you more about this.

Please make sure that you have also answered Question 9.

Other types of registration

11 Paragraph 8 of the registration booklet explains when you can apply for registration if the value of your taxable supplies is below the registration limits. If, having read this, you decide to apply, you should:

- tick the box;
- give the value of your taxable supplies in the last twelve months; **and**
- enclose a letter explaining why you want to be registered and from what date.

12 Paragraph 9 of the registration booklet explains when you can apply for registration if you are not yet making taxable supplies but intend to do so in the future. If, having read this, you decide to apply, you should:

- tick the box;
- give the annual value of taxable supplies you expect to make;
- give the approximate date when you expect to make your first taxable supply;
- enclose supporting evidence to show that you intend to make taxable supplies by that date; **and**
- enclose a letter giving the date from which you want to be registered.

Business changes and transfers

If you are answering Questions 13 and 14, you should read the leaflet *Transfer of a business as a going concern*, because of the special VAT rules which apply.

13 If you are taking a business over as a going concern, or changing the legal status of your existing business, for example from sole proprietor to partnership, you should:

- tick the box; **and**
- answer questions (a), (b) and (c).

14 Tick the box if you wish to retain the existing registration number of the business.

Related businesses

15 If, during the last twelve months, you have been (or now are) an officer (for example, director, company secretary), sole proprietor or partner of any VAT registered business, you should:

- tick the YES box; **and**
- enclose a letter giving the name(s)of the business(es) and the VAT registration number(s).

If, during the last twelve months, you have not been an officer (for example, director, company secretary), sole proprietor or partner of any VAT registered business, please tick the NO box.

Declaration

16 Only the person specified below should sign the declaration and tick the appropriate box:

- for a sole proprietor – the sole proprietor
- for a partnership – a partner
- for a company incorporated under the UK Companies Act – a director or the company secretary
- for a public corporation or nationalised body, or a local authority, or any other corporation – an authorised official
- for an unincorporated association – an authorised official
- for a trust – the trustee(s)
- for an overseas company, non-resident person or firm – see the leaflet *Overseas traders and United Kingdom VAT*.

Please remember, you must send the completed form(s), with any extra information requested, to the VAT office nearest your principal place of business.

Value Added Tax Return

For the period

to

H M Customs and Excise

Due to reach the VAT Central Unit by
These dates must not be altered.

For Official Use

Registration No | Period

Before you fill in this form please read the notes on the other side. You must complete all boxes — writing "none" where necessary.
If you need to show an exact amount of pounds, please write "00" in the pence column. Don't put a dash or leave the column blank. Please write clearly in ink.
You must ensure that the completed form and any VAT payable are received no later than the due date by the Controller, VAT Central Unit, H M Customs and Excise, 21 Victoria Avenue, SOUTHEND-ON-SEA X

An envelope is enclosed for your use.

For Official Use		
	£	p

FOR OFFICIAL USE

		£	p
VAT DUE in this period on OUTPUTS (sales, etc), certain postal imports and services received from abroad	1		
Underdeclarations of VAT made on previous returns (but not those notified in writing by Customs and Excise)	2		
TOTAL VAT DUE (box 1 + box 2)	3		
VAT DEDUCTIBLE in this period on INPUTS (purchases, etc)	4		
Overdeclarations of VAT made on previous returns (but not those notified in writing by Customs and Excise)	5		
TOTAL VAT DEDUCTIBLE (box 4 + box 5)	6		
NET VAT PAYABLE OR REPAYABLE (Difference between boxes 3 and 6)	7		

Please tick only ONE of these boxes:

box 3 greater than box 6 — payment by credit transfer — payment enclosed
box 6 greater than box 3 — repayment due

How to pay the VAT due
Cross all cheques and postal orders "A/C Payee only" and make them payable to "H M Customs and Excise". Make credit transfers through account 3078027 at National Girobank or 10-70-50 52055000 for Bank Giros and keep your payment slip. You can order pre-printed booklets of credit transfer slips from your local VAT office. In your own interest do not send notes, coins, or uncrossed postal orders through the post.
Please write your VAT registration number on the back of all cheques and credit transfer slips.

| Value of Outputs (excluding any VAT) | 8 | | |
| Value of Inputs (excluding any VAT) | 9 | | |

Please tick box(es) if the statement(s) apply:

box 5 includes bad debt relief — box 8 includes exempt outputs — box 8 includes exports
Retail schemes If you have used any of the schemes in the period covered by this return please tick the box(es) to show all the schemes used.

A | B | C | D | E | F | G | H |

Remember, you could be liable to a financial penalty if your return and all the VAT payable are not received by the due date.
DECLARATION by the signatory to be completed by or on behalf of the person named above.

I, ... declare that the
(full name of signatory in BLOCK LETTERS)
information given above is true and complete.

Signed .... Date........................ 19.
*(Proprietor, partner, director, secretary, responsible officer, committee member of club or association, duly authorised person) *Delete as necessary

FOR OFFICIAL USE

VAT 100   F3790 (October 1987)

There are currently two rates of tax:

- Standard rate – 15 per cent
- Zero rate – 0 per cent

The majority of businesses will charge VAT at the rate of 15 per cent but some businesses (eg farms, publishers) make predominantly zero-rated supplies. Consequently, their input tax frequently exceeds their output tax. Businesses of this nature regularly find repayments of tax due to them from Customs and Excise.

Certain supplies are exempt from VAT. These include supplies made by financial institutions, insurance brokers and certain educational organisations. Businesses making wholly exempt supplies cannot register for VAT. Those making some exempt and some taxable supplies may be able to register for VAT. However, businesses in this situation may find that they are unable to reclaim all the input tax which they incur on expenses.

From 1 April 1989 the VAT legislation as it relates to the construction industry and transactions in land property was altered radically. As a result, many businesses previously unaffected by VAT have now been brought into the VAT net.

The new legislation affects not only property developers but also businesses buying or selling property plus those developing property for their own occupation. Before any transactions in property are entered into, it is advisable to seek professional guidance in order to maximise planning opportunities and minimise the risk of incurring penalties.

If a potential 'taxable person', who is liable to register because he or she has exceeded the turnover limits, fails to notify Customs and Excise at the correct time, his or her registration may be backdated and the 'taxable person' may have to account for tax on turnover since that date even though that person may not have charged VAT to customers. Customs and Excise may also levy a non-mitigable penalty.

Once registered, VAT returns (Form VAT 100) are usually made quarterly, although you can apply for a monthly return period if repayments are anticipated. It will reduce the amount of accounting if you ensure that the quarterly VAT return coincides with your year end. The VAT return, together with any tax due, must be submitted within one month of the end of the period to which it relates. Heavy penalties/interest are imposed for late returns, late payment or incorrect returns.

HM Customs and Excise are also empowered to carry out 'VAT audits' to ensure that a trader is accounting for VAT correctly; full-scale investigations can be undertaken by Customs and Excise if they believe that the VAT regulations are being abused.

Letterheads, invoices and nameplates

The design of your logo and stationery can be an important part of your marketing strategy, as letters, invoices, mail shots and statements are all forms of public relations.

Company

The business letters and order forms of a company must clearly show the country of registration and number under which it is registered, the address of the registered office and the address of the place of business if it is different from the registered office. It is not essential to list the names of the directors of the company, but if they are to be specified, they must all be named. If directors are named, the nationality must be noted of those who are not EC nationals.

The name of the company must also be shown on its notices, official publications, bills of exchange, promissory notes, endorsements, cheques and orders for money or goods, invoices, receipts and letters of credit. A nameplate must also appear outside each office (including the registered office) or place of business. Invoices must state the VAT registration number.

The table on page 63 sets out the legal requirements.

Partnership

All business letters, written orders for goods or services, invoices, receipts and written demands must either clearly state the name of each partner and the address within Great Britain where any documents may be served upon him or her, or state where a list of partners may be inspected. A notice containing the names and addresses of all the partners must be predominantly displayed in any place where the partnership business is carried on. Invoices must state the VAT registration number.

Sole trader

A sole trader may carry on business under a name other than his own. It is not necessary to register the business name, although it must be shown on all business documentation, together with the address from which business is conducted. A sole trader is not obliged to put up a nameplate, but it may be advantageous to do so to inform passers-by of your existence. Invoices must state the VAT registration number.

Letterheads, invoices and nameplates

Information	Letters	Orders	Invoices	Cheques	Official publications and forms	Premises
Name of company	Yes	Yes	Yes	Yes	Yes	Yes
Country of registration	Yes	Yes				Yes
Address of registered office	Yes	Yes				Yes
Company number	Yes	Yes				
VAT number			Yes			
Forename or initials and surname (and nationality of non EC directors) of ALL or NONE of the directors	Yes	Yes				

Insurances

Before starting trading you should review the insurance cover that you require with an insurance broker.

Basically, there are two categories of cover:

Compulsory cover

A business is required to effect third-party insurance as follows:

- employer's liability – personal injury or damage to personal property of employees;
- motor insurance for all vehicles.

Voluntary cover

It is advisable to seek advice and to obtain quotations on the following additional insurances:

- public liability – personal injury or damage to personal property of the public;
- property damage – fire and theft, storm and flood water damage.
- product liability – indemnity against a product which has been manufactured, treated or repaired and causes injury or damage to a third party;
- business interruption – consequential loss of profits resulting from fire, theft etc.
- computer damage;
- bad debt cover;
- goods in transit.

Other insurances

Specialist insurances, dependent upon the business operated; for instance professional indemnity cover, should be considered.

Key man insurance should also be taken out if the business is dependent for its future on certain individuals. It may also be appropriate for the directors/proprietors to take out life assurance policies on each other.

You should note that all contracts of insurance are contracts of the utmost good faith, and therefore when completing proposal forms full disclosure must be made. Failure to observe this could render an insurance contract invalid.

6

Employing People

Good employees are valuable assets and therefore as much care and attention should be given to recruitment as to any other aspect of the business. Getting recruitment wrong can be a costly exercise, not only in terms of the time and money invested in a new employee, but also the lost performance, disruption to the business and the 'knock-on' demotivating effect on other employees. It is essential, therefore, to get recruitment right.

The employment of people carries heavy responsibilities and should not be undertaken lightly. There is extensive legislation relating to employment in general and especially to the health and safety of people at work.

Although the term 'company' has been used throughout this chapter, the regulations apply to all businesses, whatever their legal entity.

Contracts of employment

As soon as someone starts work for a business, a legal contract with that person arises, whether or not anything is written down. Within 13 weeks of employment commencing, an employer is required to provide all employees working 16 hours or more per week with a written statement of their main terms and conditions of employment. This should include:

- the name of the employer;
- job title;
- date continuous employment began;
- hours of work including overtime arrangements;
- rate and frequency of pay;
- holidays;
- sick pay arrangements;
- pension scheme (if applicable);
- length of notice required to terminate employment;
- disciplinary and grievance procedures.

A specimen statement of terms and conditions of employment is included as Appendix 6. This is not definitive and needs to be tailored to your particular needs.

Employment rights

The employee has a number of statutory rights not necessarily included in the contract of employment. Among these are:

- the minimum periods of notice as follows:

up to 2 years' service	– 1 week
2 to 12 years' service	– 1 week for each year of continuous employment
more than 12 years' service	– 12 weeks;

- the right to statutory sick pay, for up to 28 weeks;
- the right, after two years' service, not to be unfairly dismissed;
- the right not to be discriminated against, on grounds of race, sex or marital status;
- the right to equal pay for work of equal value;
- the right to continuity of terms and conditions of employment when a business is sold as a going concern;
- the right, after two years' service, to a statutory redundancy payment;
- the right to take part in trade union activities and undertake trade union duties;
- the right to maternity pay, to maternity leave and subsequently to return to work if the appropriate service qualifications have been met.
- Further details are given in Appendix 6.

Health and safety

Ultimate responsibility for the health and safety of a company's employees, and those affected by the company's activities, rests with the employer. This duty is imposed by the Health and Safety at Work Act 1974, together with various provisions of the Factories Act and Offices, Shops and Railway Premises Act. In addition, the employer must insure against liability for bodily injury or disease sustained by employees, arising out of, or in the course of, employment, in accordance with the Employers' Liability (Compulsory Insurance) Act.

Wages, tax and National Insurance

In a few industries, statutory minimum rates of pay and holidays are laid down by Wages Councils. Otherwise it is up to the company to set the rate of pay for the job, although it may be necessary to take account of whether national or local union agreements exist in the industry. The telephone numbers and addresses of the Wages Councils are given in Appendix 9.

The amount of remuneration and the manner in which it is paid are agreed between the employer and the employee. Employees are entitled to receive an itemised statement, showing gross pay, deductions and the amount of net pay.

Details of the PAYE system are given in Chapter 5, but in summary:

- The employer must deduct income tax from the employee's pay before payment under the PAYE system if the employee earns over a certain amount. If the employer fails to do so, he or she may be required to pay the tax which should have been deducted and, in addition, may be liable to penalties. The employer should tell the local tax office that he or she intends to operate the PAYE system. The tax office will issue tax codes for each of the company's employees and will send stationery and guides to show how to make the deductions.
- Employees' National Insurance contributions must also be deducted from their wages, and employer's contributions paid. Any DSS office can tell the employer how to assess and forward the sums.
- Since 6 April 1986 Statutory Sick Pay (SSP) has been payable to employees for up to 28 weeks of sickness in any one period of incapacity for work. SSP is classed as remuneration and National Insurance contributions are therefore payable by both the employer and the employee. Employers may reclaim the SSP and their National Insurance contributions by deducting the amount paid from their total National Insurance bill before remittance to the Inland Revenue. (SSP replaces the employee's entitlement to state sickness benefits for the first 28 weeks of sickness.)
- A similar system operates with respect to Statutory Maternity Pay (SMP). It is payable to the mother for a maximum of 18 weeks, during which she is not working, but is recoverable by deduction from National Insurance contributions payable.

Disciplinary rules and procedures

It is important that a company has clear and well-understood disciplinary rules and procedures. Employees should have a copy of these. By following these rules consistently and fairly when any disciplinary problem arises, a company will minimise the risk of a finding of unfair dismissal.

The unfair dismissal rules are to be found in the Employment Protection (Consolidation) Act 1978. The law provides that an employer can fairly dismiss an employee if:

- he or she has a 'fair' reason for dismissal;
- he or she has acted reasonably in taking the decision to dismiss.

'Fair' reasons

Capability
The employee is unable to do the job satisfactorily or does not have the qualifications to do the job or is physically or mentally unable through illness to do the job.

Conduct
Offences which constitute misconduct or gross misconduct, such as fighting, refusing to obey an order, stealing, drinking on duty. Conduct is the most common reason for dismissal and the one which results in the largest number of unfair dismissal complaints.

Redundancy
Where the requirement for an employee to carry out work of a particular kind ceases or diminishes. Generally, an employee does not have grounds for challenging the reason for the redundancy. However, he or she can claim for unfair selection for redundancy in preference to another employee. An employer must ensure that the selection criteria are fair and that he or she had consulted the employee and considered any suitable alternative job.

Contravention of a statutory duty or restriction
Where an employee cannot perform his or her assigned duties as a result of being statutorily barred, eg not having a work permit or losing a driving licence.

Other substantial reasons
Situations in which an employer has a good reason for dismissing an employee but where the grounds for dismissal are not included in the above four categories. An example would be where an employee has persistently refused to work under new terms and conditions following a reorganisa-

tion of a business, or where a criminal conviction outside employment has made the employee unsuitable to do the job or unacceptable to colleagues.

'Fair' procedures

The employer, apart from showing that there had been a fair reason to dismiss, must also show that he or she acted reasonably in dismissing the employee for that particular reason. This involves two questions:

- whether the procedure used to carry out the dismissal was fair, ie whether the employee was given an opportunity to state his or her case, before the decision was taken;
- whether it was reasonable in the circumstances to dismiss, having regard to all the circumstances leading up to the decision to dismiss, ie whether the employee was warned prior to being dismissed or, in the case of gross misconduct, whether the misconduct was serious enough to warrant dismissal for the first offence.

It is essential that a company develops a disciplinary procedure which embodies these principles. Employees should be aware of the circumstances in which they will be subject to disciplinary action; the action which may be taken, eg written warnings of dismissal; and who will be responsible for deciding upon the action taken.

A Code of Practice on disciplinary procedures is available from local Arbitration and Conciliation Advisory Service (ACAS) offices.

Employers commonly underestimate the time it takes them to manage their employees. Adequate time must be allowed for this important task to ensure that the business gets the best out of what is likely to be its most important asset.

7
Marketing the Product or Service

Market research

Whatever their talents, skilled craftsman, top executive, butcher or candlestick maker, all people have one thing in common when they start up a new business – no customers, no business. Many people setting up in business have a vague idea that there are lots of people out there who need them. This is a very pleasant thought and good for the ego, but it will not pay the costs of setting up and running a business and it will not convince your bank manager to lend you money. To build a business you have to persuade people either to switch their custom from another supplier or to spend their money in a different way. In either case you have to persuade them to write cheques to you rather than to somebody else, or to spend their savings.

When you are starting a business, the way to understand better whether customers really exist for your particular product or service is to ask a number of questions. Examples include:

- How many potential customers are there?
- How many real customers are there?
- Who are they?
- When is the buying done?
- What kind of products or services do they want to buy?
- Why do they want the product or service?
- Where do they get it at present?
- How much do they pay at the moment?
- How much will they pay for my product?
- What deficiencies are there in the products or services which they buy at the moment?
- When do customers buy, how much and how frequently?
- Can you deliver what they want and when they want it?
- Who else can supply this product or service?

- How strong is this competition?
- Will the market grow or contract?

To answer these questions you should:

- Carry out desk research from material published in newspapers, magazines, advertisements and market surveys. You will be surprised how much helpful information is available from the business section of good public libraries and trade associations.
- Visit potential retailers and distributors. Do remember that retailers are always looking for new and improved products so they have an interest in talking to potential new suppliers. In the case of large multiple retailers, talk to retail assistants and ask to see the store manager. When you have talked to a few people at branch level you will be much better prepared to go out and talk to the buyer at head office.
- Visit potential customers both large and small. Remember that in a small company only one person may be involved in the purchasing decision, but in a large company many people may be involved and may need to be influenced. Part of your research will be aimed at finding out how companies are organised to buy your particular product or service.
- Visit competitors. A great deal of information can be obtained from competitors just by asking. Few organisations stop to think whether someone approaching them might be a competitor. In this way you can collect samples, sales brochures and price-lists.
- Visit users and discuss the benefits and deficiencies they associate with your type of product or service. You can also take this opportunity to discuss your particular product.

Such contacts may be made by:

- personal visits, which are the best method;
- telephone, but this method can only be used by a skilled person;
- observation, particularly in the case of a would-be retailer, where traffic flows into the shop are of vital importance in deciding on an appropriate location.

The product or service

It is very easy, and bad business, to think that your new product or service has to be the cheapest. People in business are becoming increasingly aware that non-price factors are very important in designing and developing a product. People buy products for a range of complex rational and irrational reasons of which price is only one. The following list shows some of the non-price factors that should be considered when designing and developing a product:

- the physical attributes of a product;
- its design;
- performance;
- packaging;
- after sales service;
- availability;
- colour, flavour, odour, touch;
- image;
- specification;
- payment terms.

Buyers are less likely to purchase a new product because it is exactly or nearly the same as one already on the market. Somehow you have to distinguish or differentiate your product or service from its competitors. Decide whether potential customers are likely to buy a new product which is better or worse according to each of the characteristics listed above. In doing this, work out which of those characteristics are most important for the particular type of customer at whom you will be aiming.

Identifying a target market

It is very tempting for someone starting up in business to stand on top of a hill looking out over a large city and say to himself or herself 'look at all those potential customers out there, I cannot fail to get plenty of customers'. But the truth lies in a very different direction. Most of those customers have very different tastes and requirements and already have a very full choice of products and services. Additionally, you may have only limited resources and it would be very expensive to attempt to sell to all of them. By the time you have approached a small proportion you would have run out of money.

Furthermore, customers have very different ideas about furniture, clothing, cars, and in fact most other types of product. Manufacturers respond by providing a choice of goods and service different from their competitors. This is called product differentiation. But it would be impossible for every manufacturer to provide a range of goods wide enough to satisfy the needs of all the different types of customer. The way manufacturers solve this problem is to identify a group of customers with similar tastes and requirements and then design a product which meets the needs of that particular group.

Identifying a target market is one of the critical success factors in marketing and is no simple task. In technical marketing jargon it is called market segmentation.

Markets can be segmented in many different ways. They may be segmented, for example, in terms of:

- the size of the business;
- type of business;
- price of the product or service;
- geographical region;
- size and consumption pattern of the users;
- how conservative they are in trying new products or services;
- the length of time taken to make a purchasing decision and the procedure for doing this.

The purpose of market segmentation is to enable the business to identify a group of customers for which its product or service is designed and directed, and to enable it to concentrate its limited resources in marketing and selling to them.

Let us take the example of company XYZ which set up in business to sell a service. The potential for this service lay among solicitors, accountants, banks, merchant banks and industrial companies which needed to retain large volumes of bulky files and other information. The temptation was for company XYZ to aim at all the firms in all these sectors. However, a brief look at the number of firms under each category made it obvious that it would cost too much to write to them all and would take years to follow this up with telephone calls and personal visits. By carrying out a number of personal market research interviews with a selection of firms in each category and of different sizes, company XYZ was able to identify its target of medium-sized firms in one particular category. The target market identified was characterised by:

- being under considerable pressure to define more cost-effective ways of doing things;
- being unable to pass higher costs on in higher fees;
- being less conservative and more adaptable to change than the larger firms;
- having the decision-making process concentrated in the hands of only a few people in contrast to the larger firms where far more people were involved in the purchasing decision.

By identifying this target market, company XYZ was able to concentrate on a relatively small number of potential customers where it obtained sufficient test trials followed by full implementation to build a profitable business. Furthermore, by targeting medium-sized firms in this sector it avoided the mainstream of competition from its large competitors who fought each other over the prize of the even larger ones.

Selling and promotion

Having identified a target market and developed a suitable product or service, the start-up business must decide on the most cost-effective way to reach its target customers. It is reported that Lord Leverhume, the founder of Unilever, once said, 'If I could afford to employ enough salesmen to call on every home in the country, I would not use advertising.' Nowadays companies have an almost unlimited choice of media and other forms of promotion. The choice will depend on a whole range of factors, including the type of product, the number of potential customers in the target group and the costs and effectiveness of the various methods available. Listed below are 20 of the most common:

- customer sales departments
- sales agents
- telephone sales
- direct mail
- posters
- radio
- TV
- newspapers
- journals
- leaflets and brochures
- mail order
- exhibitions and shows
- party plans
- cinema
- in-store demonstrations
- window displays and showcases
- distribution of product samples
- public relations
- conferences and workshops
- promotion.

In selecting how much a business should spend and which of the above methods to use, the management would be well advised to consult a small advertising agency and/or firm of management consultants.

For example, effective participation in a well-chosen exhibition can work wonders for small, little-known businesses seeking customers.

However, common mistakes include choosing an unsuitable exhibition, underestimating the number of people and costs involved and omitting to follow up on all interested contacts after the exhibition.

In business start-ups and expansion, it is easy to overlook the workload in generating new business. If you should doubt this point, estimate the number of sales leads you need in order to generate one order. For one sale simply estimate:

- how many leads are required to generate one first interview;
- how many contacts with a named, relevant person are needed as a prelude to a first interview;
- how many first interviews you need for making a first sales presentation;
- how many second interviews you need for overcoming objections and confirming details;
- how many third interviews you need in the final bid for the business;
- your likely conversion rate.

If you make a realistic assessment, you should not be surprised if you need over 100 leads to achieve one sale. When you estimate the actual cost in terms of time, you will appreciate the workload in generating new business.

8
Managing the Business

Introduction

An efficiently run business is more likely to succeed than a business where organisation is lacking on the administrative side. In the early stages, it may seem to be an economy to attempt to deal with paperwork yourself in the evenings and at weekends, but if you let things get out of hand it will become a false economy, as your books of account and other tasks fall behind. A good bookkeeper/administrator, perhaps initially on a part-time basis, to deal with the accounting and administrative requirements of the business, is normally a sound investment.

Accounting systems

Legal requirements
The Companies Act 1985 requires that the directors of a limited company ensure that proper books of account are kept with respect to:

- all monies received and paid and the purpose to which they were applied;
- all sales and purchases by the company;
- all assets and liabilities of the company.

They are also required to prepare financial statements on an annual basis and to have these accounts audited by an independent accountant.

There are no legal requirements in respect of accounting records for an unincorporated business other than to supply annual financial statements to the Inland Revenue which can be supported by documentary evidence, and the maintenance of the appropriate records for PAYE and VAT purposes if the business is registered. However, in practical terms the accounting requirements of all businesses are similar.

Management requirements

It is important that the proprietors establish a sound and informative accounting system, not only for statutory purposes but also for their own commercial purposes. There is no doubt that the more successful businesses are those where the proprietors are made aware of the company's financial position on a regular basis.

The accounting system

The accounting system adopted by the business should therefore be designed to provide the information and controls required by the Companies Act 1985 (where applicable), HM Customs and Excise (who administer VAT) and the Inland Revenue (for PAYE, income and corporation tax purposes). The sophistication of the system will depend on individual requirements but it will, in any case, establish the flow of documents, and their filing and retrieval within the system. In general, it is advisable to keep your systems as simple and straightforward as possible.

A standard set of books of account would comprise:

- *Cash Book* – to record receipts and payments through the bank accounts.
- *Petty cash book* – to record payments of a smaller nature in cash. It is usual for cash receipts to be banked along with cheques.
- *Purchase day book* – an analysed list of invoices from suppliers.
- *Purchase ledger* – a record of the amounts owed to suppliers.
- *Sales day book* – an analysed list of your sales invoices.
- *Sales ledger* – a record of amounts owed by your debtors.
- *Control accounts* – total accounts for the cash and petty cash books and for the sales and purchase ledgers which enable you to double check that all the entries have been made correctly.
- *Wages book/deduction sheets* – individual and total payroll records.
- *Register of fixed assets* – a listing of plant, equipment, cars and other fixed assets to enable their existence and insurance to be controlled.
- *Nominal ledger* – the principal book, in which entries are made in total from other books listed above, and from which accounts are prepared.

The books of account are where the transactions of the business are recorded when the paperwork involved has been processed. Systems are also required for:

- dealing with ordering goods or services, checking their receipt and dealing with the recording and payment of purchase invoices;

- receiving and processing customers' orders, despatching goods, invoicing out sales and receiving payment;
- controlling the workforce and the hours worked;
- controlling the movement of stock; and
- producing regular management information.

Computers

Many of the above books of account can be maintained on a computer, which is worth considering at the outset if you anticipate that large volumes will necessitate this at an early date. It is far easier to set up and become familiar with a computer system while volume is still comparatively small, than to transfer large quantities of data later, which can be time-consuming and costly. There are many computer systems on the market which can be expanded as the business grows by adding additional equipment or increasing the capacity of existing equipment without having to discard any of the initial system purchased. Even if you do not use a computer to start with, it may be worth bearing possible computerisation in mind when designing your accounting system, so that the computer (when you get it) will fit into your existing office routines, rather than causing disruption to your staff and the systems that they are used to operating.

Accounting disciplines

Sales invoicing

Prompt invoicing of sales is the first requirement of good cash control. A customer usually takes credit by delaying payment to his supplier and this period will only commence when he approves the invoice.

Banking of cash received

Prompt banking of cash received is the next requirement. All cheques should be banked on the day they are received, as should amounts received in cash. You should avoid using cash receipts to replenish your petty cash or as drawings, as this will eventually catch up with you when you forget to enter it in the accounting system and then chase a customer who has already paid you.

Bank and cash reconciliations

Regular (at least monthly) totalling of your cash books, and reconciliations with bank statements or cash in hand as appropriate, will quickly identify any errors. Regular reconciliations will mean that you rely on the balances shown in your cash books which will help you to monitor your cash flow.

Control accounts

Regular reconciliation of control or total accounts to the list of balances in the appropriate ledgers enable errors to be found more easily, since the error can only have occurred since the last reconciliation. If that was a year ago, tracing the error will be time-consuming!

Credit control

Cash is the lifeblood of any business. The chasing of outstanding debts is one of the most important functions in a business and uses the information in your sales ledger, which must therefore be kept up to date. Efficient credit control will ensure that your cash flow is maintained, and you can continue in business. There is no point in selling goods or services if you do not get paid for them. A telephone call will often suffice to collect a debt from a slow payer, and a 'softly, softly' approach will sometimes be more effective than a threatening letter. However, whatever method you adopt you must keep the pressure on your customers to pay.

Stock control

It is important to implement a stock control system in order to:

- provide details of what is in stock at any period of time;
- identify when stock needs to be reordered;
- identify overstocking, slow-moving or obsolete stock;
- provide information to arrive at the value of your stock for accounting purposes.

Ordering of goods

You need to establish a system for placing orders with suppliers, monitoring the receipt and quality of those goods or services, accounting for the purchase in your books of account and finally paying the invoice.

Filing systems

The basic rules are to open a file when it is needed, and to file all completed paperwork as soon as possible.

Five categories of filing should suffice:

- *Office* – personnel, advertising, insurance, general correspondence
- *Legal* – contracts, leases etc.

- *Accounting* – purchase and sales invoices, payment vouchers, bank statements etc.
- *Equipment* – plant, office furniture and equipment, motor vehicles.
- *Sales* – customers' correspondence, price-lists, competitors' price-lists etc.

Company administration

The importance of the company's statutory records should not be underestimated; they are definitive proof of the company's legal existence and of its memory. The records that should be kept are:

- register of shareholders;
- minutes of directors' and shareholders' meetings;
- register of directors and secretaries;
- register of charges;
- register of directors' interests in shares;
- register of share or stock transfers;
- register of debenture holders;
- copies of directors' service contracts.

Management accounts/budgets

In Chapter 2 we described the preparation of the business plan to set your objectives and determine the level of finance you require. However, this must not be seen as a one-off exercise. Good planning and budgeting are ongoing requirements if the business is to survive and grow.

In order to manage the business effectively you must use the accounting and administrative systems described in this chapter to prepare regular (usually monthly) management accounts and compare these accounts with your original budgets.

Many businesses fail because the management do not have a financial handle on where their business is going. If, for example, your sales are 50 per cent lower than those budgeted, or your expenses are 20 per cent higher than anticipated, then the level of cash you require will increase. Equally, your business might be more successful than originally envisaged. In either case you will probably need to refer back to your bank for additional finance. The bank manager will not be prepared to advance further funds unless he understands fully the position of the business and the exact reasons why the problem has arisen.

It is essential to realise that management accounts are prepared not only for your bank manager/investor but more importantly to enable you to run the business on a day-to-day basis. In Appendix 8 is detailed a simple format for the comparison of monthly accounting information with the budgets prepared by the company. The variances on both a monthly and cumulative basis should be analysed carefully so that you can identify how they have arisen and take corrective action as appropriate.

Most of the items in the monthly accounting package are self-descriptive, but you will need to bear in mind the following.

Depreciation

The assets you purchase to run your business (motor vehicles, plant and machinery etc) have a finite life. It is necessary to write off those assets against your profit and loss account by way of charging depreciation. For example, if you buy a motor van now for £5000 and it has a life of four years, you should charge £1250 to the profit and loss account each year, representing the cost to you of using that vehicle.

Stock

Stock should be valued at the month end at the cost to you. However, if you are not able to sell it at cost (eg it becomes obsolete) then you should value it at realisable value. It may not always be possible to count every item of stock at every month end to determine its value, but it is imperative to make as accurate an assessment as you can on a monthly basis and then verify the figures, say every quarter, by carrying out a full stocktake. Management frequently find that when they are preparing their year end accounts they have been wrongly estimating stocks at month ends and therefore have been obtaining inaccurate information on how the business is going.

Gross profit

When preparing the original budgets you would have determined the mark-up on your goods. The mark-up is the difference between the price at which you sell goods and their cost to you. The extent to which you are achieving your budgeted mark-up can be determined by comparing the percentage relationship between your sales and your gross profit (shown in Appendix 8 as 'gross profit percentage'). If there is a wide divergence between actual and budgeted results, you need to investigate immediately to determine the cause (eg is your sale price correct?; are the goods costing you more than anticipated?; is there an error in your accounting?).

Other overheads

Overheads need to be watched on a regular basis. Many businesses control and achieve their gross profit levels only to have them dissipated by overspending on expenses.

Working capital
You will frequently hear the term 'working capital' which in simple terms
is the difference between your current assets and your current liabilities
(Appendix 8, balance sheet line D). Current assets are items such as cash
plus stock and other assets which will be converted into cash within one
year. Current liabilities are debts which are due to be paid within one year.

Break-even
As mentioned earlier in this book, understanding the business's break-even
point is a useful management tool. In order to identify the break-even
point of the business two further concepts need to be understood:

Variable costs	are those which change depending on the value of sales and production (eg purchase of materials, direct labour costs).
Fixed costs	are those which remain the same whatever the level of sales and production (eg rent, rates, management salaries).

The break-even point is calculated using the formula:

$$\frac{\text{Total fixed costs}}{\text{Selling price} - \text{variable cost per unit}}$$

For example, assume the following figures are extracted from a company's
budgets:

	Budget £	Fixed £	Variable £
Sales	200,000	–	200,000
Cost of manufacture	110,000	–	110,000
Cost of distribution	10,000	–	10,000
Cost of selling	30,000	–	30,000
Cost of administration	15,000	15,000	–
Cost of financing	5,000	5,000	–
	170,000	20,000	150,000
Net profit	30,000		

Budgeted sales volume is 10,000 items selling at a price of £20 each.

It is apparent from the above information that the variable cost per unit is:

$$\frac{£150,000}{10,000} = £15 \text{ per unit}$$

Using the formula above the break-even point is:

$$\frac{£20,000 \text{ (total fixed costs)}}{£20 \text{ (selling price)} - £15 \text{ (variable cost per unit)}} = 4,000 \text{ units}$$

Therefore, based on this budget, the business must sell at least 4,000 units at a selling price of £20 each to cover the total costs to the company.

The figures can be proved as follows:

	Budget (10,000 units) £		Break-even (4,000 units) £	
Sales	200,000	(100%)	80,000	(100%)
Variable costs	150,000	(75%)	60,000	(75%)
Contribution to overheads	50,000		20,000	
Fixed overheads	20,000		20,000	
Net profit	30,000		Nil	

- the percentage relationship between sales and variable costs is the same for the budget and break-even results;
- the same break-even result gives neither profit nor loss.

Conclusion

Many people running businesses concentrate on the selling and production side and give no thought to the financial implications of what they are doing. A good accounting and administration system will give you the management tools to make valid business decisions and help your business grow.

Auditors/accountants

Limited companies

Under the Companies Act 1985 a limited company is required to have its accounts audited on an annual basis by an independent accountant. The accountant is required to review the accounts and the systems used, and to state whether these accounts give 'a true and fair view' of the state of affairs and results of the business at a point in time.

Sole traders/Partnerships

In relation to sole traders and partnerships an accountant is usually engaged to prepare periodic (annual) accounts.

For all business entities it is usual for the accountant to deal on behalf of the business with the Inland Revenue to agree corporation and/or income tax liabilities.

General advice

It is important that you obtain sound professional advice at the outset of your business. It is likely that the accountant will have been involved in assisting you in preparing your business plan but you should seek advice, among other things, on:

- the bookkeeping system most appropriate to your circumstances;
- VAT and PAYE registration and systems;
- preparation of regular management information and interpretation of results;
- general business matters.

9
Providing for the Future

Introduction

Whether an individual is in business as a sole trader, in partnership or is running a limited company it is important to plan a pension for the future. It is worth bearing in mind that a male retiring at the age of 60 has an average life expectancy of approximately 21 years. A pension will therefore be expected to provide an adequate level of income for approximately a quarter of a person's lifetime. In short, a pension is the most important investment an individual will make apart from his or her own business.

The tax and legal framework governing pension provision, for the self-employed and those in employment where no pension is provided, differs from that for employees provided with pensions by their employers. The legislation in relation to pensions has been changed substantially in the last five years. Sound, independent professional advice is essential before entering into any pension arrangements.

Pension provision

The following provisions are for the self-employed and those not provided with a pension by their employers.

Personal pension schemes
Individuals who are self-employed or are not provided with a pension by their employer may invest a proportion of their net relevant earnings (ie earnings after the expenses of the business but before personal tax allowances or tax have been deducted). Up to the age of 35 this proportion is 17.5 per cent and it increases with age to a maximum of 40 per cent for individuals aged between 61 and 74. Personal pension schemes supersede, from 1 July 1988, what used to be called retirement annuity policies (RAPs). Anyone who has an RAP should take professional advice before

85

changing his or her pension arrangements. Under the new personal pension scheme legislation, banks, building societies and unit trust groups may also market personal pension schemes in addition to life assurance companies, subject to compliance with the new legislation.

The premiums paid (up to the statutory limits) are deductible from income for tax purposes and, once invested, accumulate in a tax exempt fund. At retirement you may take up to 25 per cent of the accumulated fund as a tax free cash sum and the balance of the fund must be used to purchase a pension which will be taxed under PAYE. You may take the benefits at any age from 50 onwards and need not retire in order to do so. The latest age at which benefits may be taken is 75.

The purpose of paying personal pension scheme premiums is to provide a pension on retirement where the premiums are invested in an investment scheme which enjoys substantial tax benefits as outlined above.

Types of policy
There are four broad categories of scheme in which you can invest:

- *Non-profit policies* which give a guaranteed return unaffected by future investment conditions. These are now rarely used but may possibly be of benefit for people very near to retirement with little time for their investment to grow.
- *With profit policies* which operate on the basis of profits or bonuses being added at periodic intervals which, once added, form part of the policy. In addition further bonuses are usually payable at the date benefits are taken to reflect investment returns over the term of the policy.
- *Unit-linked policies* where the premium paid by the individual purchases units in one of a range of funds offered by the personal pension scheme provider. Once invested, the unit values reflect the underlying value of the funds in which they are invested.
- *Deposit administration policies* which work on the basis that premiums are invested in a deposit fund often linked to fixed interest rates or building society lending rates.

Individual circumstances will dictate what type of policy or combination of policies is likely to be most appropriate, though it is usual for most people to effect a combination of with profit and unit linked policies.

For employees, pension benefits are as follows:

Retirement benefit schemes
An employer may provide pension benefits for employees by setting up a scheme which provides:

- a maximum of two-thirds of the final salary as long as the employee has at least 20 years' service and subject to a maximum pension of £40,000, ie two-thirds of £60,000 (which is now the upper limit for exempt approved schemes following the Finance Act 1989). The £60,000 limit is to be increased annually by the Retail Price Index;
- a maximum spouse's pension of two-thirds of the employee's pension payable to the spouse or dependant, in the event of predeceasing the spouse after retirement;
- lump sum life assurance cover of up to four times the salary at the date of death if an employee dies before retirement.
- Spouse's and dependant's pensions of up to two-thirds of the employee's salary at the date of death if he or she dies before retirement.

Payments in respect of the above will often be made by the employer to a life assurance company if the scheme has less than, say, 50 to 75 members; the employee may contribute up to 15 per cent of salary by way of Additional Voluntary Contributions (AVCs) and obtain tax relief at his or her highest marginal rate. Employees may also pay Free Standing AVCs (FSAVCs) to pension providers of their own choice subject again to a 15 per cent of salary limit.

Personal pension schemes

As an alternative, an employer can contribute to an employee's personal pension scheme. The contribution limits (17.5 to 40 per cent depending on age) apply whether contributions are made by the employer or employee alone or in combination.

Small self-administered pension schemes

The employer may also consider establishing a small self-administered pension scheme (SSAS) for the directors and senior executives of the company. Under these schemes (for firms which must have 12 or fewer employees) the company pays premiums to the SSAS and these funds are then invested for the benefit of the members of the scheme (ie the employees, including directors) and can be invested in a range of approved assets such as equities and property as well as insurance company funds. The maximum benefits are the same as for employees in a retirement benefits scheme.

Loan facilities

Based on monies paid into a fund and anticipated benefits, the employee may obtain loan facilities. This is particularly useful in respect of mortgages which can be linked to pension premiums being paid. It is important to note that the policy or plan cannot under law be assigned. Instead, the lender accepts the pension plan as evidence of the ability to repay the mortgage at retirement. The lender will still usually require an assignment over a life assurance policy in order to ensure that the loan is repaid in the event of death before retirement. A charge over the property will also be required in the normal way.

Conclusion

In summary, planning can provide for an individual, together with his or her spouse and dependants, not only a pension during retirement but also valuable life benefits payable on death before retirement. In addition, the tax-free cash sum may be used to obtain tax-efficient mortgage facilities.

For these reasons any person in business should give serious consideration to making appropriate pension arrangements at an early age.

10
Obtaining Assistance

A large number of people and professional bodies are able to give advice and assistance to small growing businesses. It is common sense to use an outsider for a particular matter when your business needs that expertise but is not able to have a suitable person on the payroll.

The proprietor will often attempt to cover too many areas, spending a disproportionate amount of time on one thing to the detriment of the enterprise as a whole. This chapter, therefore, summarises the help and advice available. Appendix 9 lists a selection of the names, addresses and telephone numbers of those who are available to help you.

Accountants

In many small businesses, the accountant comes once a year to prepare annual accounts, and audit them if they are for a company. The only other time an accountant will be contacted will be if the business is in difficulties, either with the VAT or tax authorities, or with the bank.

There are, however, a wide range of other services which are available from firms of accountants. These include:

- advice on the best type of trading entity for your business, taking into account your own personal circumstances and any legal or professional requirements;
- organising the legal registration of a company or advising on a partnership agreement;
- designing and setting up suitable accounting and bookkeeping systems for the business and helping to monitor the information;
- writing up the books (or processing the accounting information on computer);
- dealing with payroll preparation and annual PAYE returns;
- assisting in the preparation of budgets and cash flow forecasts for

internal use as well as in connection with applications for bank facilities, and attending meetings with your bank manager;

- advising on possible sources of finance, and helping with the preparation of a business plan to achieve the financing required;
- advising on grants available when setting up or expanding your business;
- advising on the taxation aspects of your business and dealing with the Inland Revenue as agent on all matters to do with taxation.

Different firms of accountants have different services to offer, and it is advisable to look around at several before choosing one to use. It is also worth bearing in mind that a larger firm will probably have greater expertise, whereas a smaller firm will probably offer a more personal service.

Solicitors

In a practical sense your accountant and lawyer will often work together to assist you. The solicitors will be able to offer you advice on:

Structure

When you have decided, in conjunction with your accountant, what legal form your business should take, a solicitor should be consulted if anything out of the ordinary is required: for instance, a company with different types of share capital or a partnership where a written agreement is needed to formalise the arrangements.

Property

Almost all firms of solicitors have expertise in property matters, and assistance with understanding contracts and leases is essential, particularly in determining your liability with regard to dilapidations, repairs and improvements.

Trading contracts

Many businesses do not require formal contracts with their customers, but even the terms of trade printed on your documentation can constitute a legal contract, and it is as well to ensure that these are checked by a solicitor. For businesses with complicated delivery dates and payment arrangements, it is even more important that the contract should be legally watertight.

Debt collection

A solicitor's letter to a slow payer will often lead to recovery of the debt, but this course should only be followed where others have failed and if you are prepared to take the debtor to court if necessary. Using solicitors for debt collection is expensive, and is not an alternative to efficient credit control. If you frequently require a debt collection service, there are specialist agencies (members of the Collection Agencies Association) whose names are in the local library, Yellow Pages and Citizens' Advice Bureau.

Litigation
If you need to sue someone, or are yourself sued, you will need the specialist services of a solicitor and also, in many instances, a barrister. Taking a case to court is very expensive, and a great number of cases are settled out of court by agreement between the parties through their lawyers.

Employment
Employment law is complex and advice should be sought, particularly in relation to contracts of service and dismissal procedures.

Other matters
Other matters which may require specialist legal advice are patents, franchises, foreign law and insolvency.

The Law Society
The Law Society publishes lists of solicitors on a regional basis, and states the type of work they are prepared to undertake, but as these lists are only of firms prepared to do legal aid work (mainly domestic and social claims) they are not exhaustive. Recommendations from colleagues, friends, your bank manager or accountant may also be useful. It is quite usual for people to use different firms for different types of work, depending on the experience and expertise required.

Bank manager

Your bank manager is an excellent source of general business advice. The experience and accessibility of the bank manager is an important criterion in choosing a bank.

In addition, some banks have set up special departments offering service to businesses. Each bank has a different way of dealing with the matter, but all have booklets setting out what facilities they have on offer to attract customers. Many of these booklets are aimed at the person wishing to set up in business.

In general, the more your bank manager knows about you and your business, the more likely he will be able to assist with your financial requirements. Regular meetings and the provision of regular financial information to your manager will help to identify when you will need increased facilities or a loan from the bank, so that the necessary arrangements can be made in advance.

If a cash flow crisis develops unexpectedly, the manager is likely to be more sympathetic and helpful to a well organised and forward looking customer, than to one whose business lurches from crisis to crisis.

Local authorities

Councils can provide help where they consider it will be of direct local benefit. They can provide mortgages of up to 90 per cent to buy land or carry out work on it. Local authorities can also provide improvement grants, prepare sites for industrial use, build new factory units and give employment subsidies.

Before starting your business you should contact your local authority, which will probably have an Industrial Development Officer or a Business Advisory Department, to find out what help is available in your area.

The Rural Development Commission

This has absorbed the Council for Small Industries in Rural Areas which was founded in 1909 to fight the large-scale unemployment caused by the new technology of that era – farm machinery that reduced the need for human labour.

The Rural Development Commission is responsible for new purpose-built factory units in the countryside; it also provides business advice, consultancy, management and technical training, as well as loans and grants for buildings, plant and equipment. It operates only in English towns with a population of 10,000 or less.

Development agencies and boards

These are geographically based, notably in Northern Ireland, Wales and Scotland, which has a national agency as well as the Highlands and Islands Development Board. Northern Ireland also has the local Enterprise Development Unit (LEDU).

Small Firms Service

This was established in 1971. It operates from 13 centres in major cities in the UK and can be reached by telephone by calling the operator on 100 and asking for Freefone Enterprise. As well as providing information, it is a useful counselling service.

The Business Counselling Service is heavily subsidised. After an initial free session with one of the counsellors (usually retired people with experience in large companies or their own businesses) there is a reasonable charge for subsequent sessions. The service is not intended as a long-term support for the management of the enterprise, but to help the entrepreneur to understand the basis of management, and to analyse the problems and work out solutions.

The Small Firms Service publishes a number of booklets on different problems that arise in the running of a business, and all contain recommended additional reading and details of useful organisations.

English Estates

This organisation develops and markets property. It usually works with local authorities or similar bodies, but also offers a professional design and build service for individuals. Mortgages are available at favourable rates.

New towns

These offer special aid in addition to any assisted area support. There are 13 in England, five in Scotland and two in Wales.

Urban Development Corporations

Urban Development Corporations were set up to revive the derelict docklands of London, Liverpool, Trafford Park, the Black Country, Cleveland, Tyne and Wear, Bristol, Leeds, Manchester and Sheffield. They have the same powers as local authorities to provide loans and grants under urban legislation.

Freeports

Freeports can be useful for maximising cash flow by storing imported raw materials until they are needed, thus avoiding paying all the VAT 'up front'.

Enterprise Agencies

These are sponsored by government, local authorities, trade associations and local companies. Their role is more advisory than financial, but they can help with many things such as marketing information, plants and sites, local costs and facilities.

Chambers of Commerce

Most large towns have a Chamber of Commerce comprising local businesses who may be contacted as a source of local information.

New Enterprise Programmes

Aimed at people starting up their own businesses, the Training Services Division of the Manpower Services Commission runs four-week residential courses, followed by 12-week non-residential courses. All fees and residential costs are met by the MSC and there is a maintenance allowance available.

Enterprise Allowance Scheme

A sum of £40 per week for 52 weeks is paid to supplement the receipts of a new business provided it has been set up by a person receiving unemployment or supplementary benefit and who has been out of work for at least eight weeks. £1000 must also be invested by the individual.

Specific Trade Advisory Services

Your trade may be such that an independent trade advisory service exists which may provide useful information and brochures.

Further contacts and addresses are given in Appendix 9.

The Enterprise Initiative

On 12 January 1988 the Department of Trade and Industry launched its Enterprise Initiative which brings together the services provided by the DTI to help small and medium-sized businesses improve their competitiveness. The principal elements of the Enterprise Initiative are:

- *The Consultancy Initiative*. Subsidised consultancy on business planning, marketing, design, quality, manufacturing and financial and information systems (see below).

- *The Regional Initiative.* In Assisted Areas and Urban Programme Areas firms can qualify for special help in relation to grants and consultancy assistance.
- *The Export Initiative.* Help in planning research and making contacts in overseas markets.
- *The Research and Technology Initiative.* Information and support for collaboration with other businesses in projects which should be aimed at creating new products and processes with commercial potential.
- *The Business and Education Initiative.* Involving businesses working more closely with schools, colleges and universities, to assist them to acquire useful skills and develop the enterprise culture in Britain. In return, businesses will gain access to the help, research and resources in higher education.

The Consultancy Initiative consists of:

- *The Business Planning Initiative.* Help in planning properly to identify and meet individual business needs.
- *The Marketing Initiative.* Assistance on market research, promotion and selling.
- *The Design Initiative.* Advice on design from product concept to corporate image.
- *The Quality Initiative.* Advice on the introduction of quality management systems which meet the right standards for the business.
- *The Manufacturing Initiative.* Advice on manufacturing strategy and the introduction of modern methods and systems.
- *The Financial and Information Initiative.* Advice on improving existing financial and budgeting systems or planning, introducing and operating new facilities.

Individuals, single companies, partnerships, parts of groups based in Great Britain with fewer than 500 employees worldwide, are eligible for these initiatives. Assistance is given in two stages, beginning with a free business review carried out by a DTI Enterprise Counsellor. The DTI will then pay half the cost of 5 to 15 man days of consultancy from a suitable expert. In Assisted Areas and Urban Programme Areas the DTI will pay two-thirds of the cost.

The Department of Trade and Industry has issued a booklet entitled 'The Enterprise Initiative', which gives details of all the individual initiatives and includes a map of Development, Intermediate and Urban Programme Areas. Copies of the booklet are available by telephoning 0800 500 200. If you require further information on the initiatives you should telephone your local contact point listed in Appendix 9, Item 30.

Appendices

Appendix 1

Business Plan: Suggested Contents

1. EXECUTIVE SUMMARY
2. CORPORATE OBJECTIVES
3. HISTORY
4. PRODUCTS OR SERVICES
5. MARKET AND MARKET STRATEGY
   - (a) customers;
   - (b) market size and trends;
   - (c) competition;
   - (d) estimated market share;
   - (e) market strategy.
6. RESEARCH AND DEVELOPMENT
7. MANAGEMENT
8. BASIS OF OPERATION
9. FINANCIAL INFORMATION
10. FINANCE REQUIRED AND ITS APPLICATION
11. PRINCIPAL RISKS AND PROBLEMS
12. LONGER-TERM OBJECTIVES

Appendices

A. DETAILED PROJECTIONS
B. ASSUMPTIONS
C. MANAGEMENT
D. PRODUCT LITERATURE ETC.

Appendix 2

Specimen Budget for the year ending.......

All in £000s		Jan	Feb	March	April
Sales	A				
Less:					
Cost of sales (opening stock plus purchases less closing stock)	B				
Gross profit (A–B)	C				
Gross profit % (C/A × 100%)					
Overheads					
Salaries and wages					
Directors' remuneration					
Depreciation					
Light, heat and power					
Repairs and renewals					
Rent and rates					
Travelling and entertaining					
Advertising					
Bank interest and charges					
General expenses					
Total overheads	D				
Net profit (C–D)	E				
Net profit % (E/A × 100%)					

May	*June*	*July*	*Aug*	*Sept*	*Oct*	*Nov*	*Dec*	*Total*

Appendix 3

Specimen Cash Flow for the year ending.......

All in £000s	Jan	Feb	March	April
Receipts				
Sales				
Sundry receipts				
A				
Payments				
Purchases				
Employees' salary and wages				
Directors' remuneration				
PAYE				
VAT				
Rent and rates				
Light, heat and power				
Repairs and renewals				
Travelling and entertaining				
Bank interest and charges				
Advertising				
General expenses				
B				
Net inflow/(outflow) (A–B)				
Balance at beginning of month				
Balance at end of month				

May	*June*	*July*	*Aug*	*Sept*	*Oct*	*Nov*	*Dec*	*Total*

Appendix 4

Specimen Balance Sheets at month end.......

All in £000s		Jan	Feb	March	April
FIXED ASSETS Freehold/leasehold property Plant and machinery, motor vehicles					
	A				
CURRENT ASSETS Stock and work in progress Debtors Cash at bank and in hand					
	B				
CURRENT LIABILITIES Creditors Bank overdraft					
	C				
NET CURRENT ASSETS (B–C)	D				
LIABILITIES PAYABLE IN MORE THAN ONE YEAR	E				
NET ASSETS (A+D–E)	F				
Share capital/ Proprietor's undrawn profit Profit retained in the business					
Note that F=G	G				

May	June	July	Aug	Sept	Oct	Nov	Dec

Appendix 5

Main Forms Used for PAYE/NIC Purposes

Form P11 (Deductions working sheet)
The deductions working sheet is used to record for each employee details of pay, tax, National Insurance contributions, Statutory Sick Pay and Statutory Maternity Pay for each period during a tax year.

It is most important that amended codes are noted on the deductions working sheet as soon as they are received from the PAYE tax office to ensure that they are implemented for the next pay period.

Form P46 (Particulars of employee for whom no code has been notified to the employer)
Form P46 should be completed if either:

(a) a new employee does not produce a Form P45; or
(b) the pay of an existing employee rises above the PAYE threshold.

The P46 procedure is a vital part of the Inland Revenue's effort to deal with the black economy. It is understood that on their visits to employers PAYE audit teams have instructions to ensure that Form P46 has been completed where necessary.

The Inland Revenue do not consider that completing a Form P46 retrospectively frees the employer from liability. If, therefore, the employee has been paid emoluments without deducting tax, the employer is liable to account for tax at the basic rate on the emoluments paid.

Form P15 (Coding claim)
Form P15 is used to provide the Inland Revenue with the information necessary to enable them to issue a notice of coding so that the correct amount of tax is deducted under the PAYE scheme from the employee's remuneration during the tax year. It is only needed when this is the employee's first employment or when he or she cannot produce a Form P45 from his or her previous employment.

Form P45 (Details of employee leaving)
Form P45 is used to summarise details of an employee's pay and tax deducted up

to the date of leaving the employment, as detailed on the employer's deductions working sheet, Form P11. The form does not require any details of National Insurance contributions, or Statutory Sick Pay – these details are subsequently included on Form P14 (see below).

If the employer makes payments to the employee after Form P45 has been issued, tax should be deducted at the basic rate from the full amount with no relief for allowances etc. Details of such payments should be included on Form P14.

If the employer makes a lump sum payment (eg a golden handshake) in connection with the cessation of the employment, it may be that only the amount by which the payment exceeds £30,000 will be treated as pay and, where appropriate, PAYE will be applied to the excess.

There are no provisions enabling employers to use substitute Forms P45, although employers with computerised payroll systems may use Forms P45 (continuous) which have been adapted for use with such systems. If an employer wishes to adopt this procedure, he or she should contact the local PAYE tax office.

The employer is not allowed to issue a duplicate Form P45 to an employee who loses the form. It will be necessary in these circumstances for the new employer to use the P46 procedure.

A retiring employee is treated as ceasing employment and a Form P45 should be issued, except where the retiring employee is to receive a pension from the employer. (In that case, Form P160 should be completed.) Note that this does not extend to pensions from the employer's pension scheme where a Form P45 should be completed in the usual way.

Forms P14, P60 (End of year return and employer's certificate: pay, tax and National Insurance contributions)

This form is a three-part form – a top copy and two carbon copies. Part 1 (the DSS copy) and Part 2 (the Inland Revenue copy) – which together comprise Form P14 – are submitted to the Collector of Taxes. Part 3 of the form constitutes Form P60 which is handed to the employee.

The forms summarise the pay, tax and National Insurance contributions and Statutory Sick Pay details for each employee for the tax year.

Many employers operate a mechanised or computer-based salaries or wages system. Such employers may seek Inland Revenue approval for the use of a substitute pre-printed three-part document. If the employer wishes to adopt this system rather than use the Inland Revenue forms, he or she should contact the local PAYE tax office.

Form P35 (Employer's annual statement)

Form P35 is used to summarise for the Inland Revenue details of tax, National Insurance contributions, Statutory Sick Pay and Statutory Maternity Pay for each employee in a tax year, and also to provide certain specific information relating to employees and others.

It should be noted that Form P35 has been designed to highlight likely weaknesses in the employer's PAYE system, and you should be aware that the Inland Revenue PAYE audit section may be alerted to any weaknesses.

Appendix 6

Specimen Statement of Terms and Conditions of Employment

STATEMENT OF TERMS AND CONDITIONS PURSUANT TO
SECTION 1
OF THE EMPLOYMENT PROTECTION (CONSOLIDATION) ACT 1978

———————————— Limited

1. Statement of terms and conditions

This statement sets out, in accordance with the provisions of the Employment Protection (Consolidation) Act 1978, the terms and conditions under which you are employed by [   ] Limited ('the Company').

Name: [   ]
Address: [   ] Job title: [   ]

2. Terms and conditions

The terms and conditions set out in this statement are to be read in conjunction with any special terms and conditions set out in any offer letter of employment sent to you by the Company. If any individual term or condition in such a letter is inconsistent with this statement, then the terms or conditions set out in the letter shall prevail unless it is contrary to any legal requirement.

3. Salary

Your current basic salary is £[   ] per year, one twelfth of which will be paid on the last day of each calendar month in respect of that month. Salary payments are subject to the normal tax and National Insurance deductions. Payment will be made by credit transfer into the bank account which you have specified.

Your salary will be reviewed at regular intervals, and you will be advised in writing of any salary increase awarded to you.

4. Commencement of employment

Your period of continuous employment with the company began on [19xx].

5. Job title and location

You are employed as [   ] and your place of work is initially
[   ] but you are liable to serve at such other place of employment as
the Company may reasonably specify to you in writing.

6. Hours of work

You are obliged to work from Monday to Friday inclusive, and your normal
hours of work are from [   ]am to [   ]pm. You are allowed one hour for
lunch, to be taken at your own discretion between the hours of 12 midday and
2 pm unless otherwise instructed.

7. Overtime

No overtime will be paid unless the Company, in its absolute discretion, agrees
otherwise. If overtime is paid, the Company shall inform you in writing of the
basis on which overtime is payable, and the rate of pay applicable.

8. Holidays

You are entitled to the usual public holidays, for which you will receive your
normal basic pay.

The Company's holiday year is the 12 months to [   ] and you are
entitled to holidays with full pay on [   ] working days per year. Your holiday
entitlement for 19xx is [   ] working days, which must be taken during that
year. Any unused entitlement may not be carried forward, and will be forfeited
unless otherwise agreed by the Company, at the Company's absolute discretion.

For any period of service with the Company less than a full holiday year, you
will receive a proportionate holiday entitlement calculated on the basis of your
entitlement for that year if served in full.

9. Absence and sickness

You will be entitled to receive your normal rate of remuneration for any periods
of sickness absence up to one month. This sum will include your statutory sick pay
entitlement in accordance with the Social Security and Housing Benefits Act 1982
and Statutory Sick Pay Regulations. Thereafter, you will be entitled only to sick
pay under SSP Regulations.

In the event of such absence you, or someone acting for you, should notify the
company as soon as possible. On returning to work you will be required to
complete a self-certification form. If the absence is for more than seven days a
doctor's note is required.

10. Notice of termination of employment

    (a) The following gives the minimum period of termination of employment
        to be given by the Company:
        (i)   after more than four weeks but less than two years of continuous
            service – 1 week;

(ii)   thereafter and until the end of 12 years of continuous service – 1 week for each year of continuous service;

(iii)   Thereafter – 12 weeks.

(b)   The minimum period of notice of termination of employment to be given by you to the Company after you have completed four weeks' continuous services shall be [   ].

11. Pensions

There is currently no pension scheme in operation in relation to your employment. The Company may, however, establish a pension scheme for its employees but it is not bound to do so. If such a scheme is established by the Company, you shall participate on such terms as the Company, at its sole discretion, shall determine from time to time.

12. Disciplinary rules and grievance procedure

If the Company is given cause for dissatisfaction with your service, you will be advised by your immediate superior of the reasons for dissatisfaction and warned that continued dissatisfaction may lead to ultimate termination of your contract. This warning will be confirmed to you in writing within five days. The written confirmation will contain details of the reasons for dissatisfaction and will specify a time period within which your service is to improve. At the end of the specified period, your service will again be reviewed and, in the event of the Company's continued dissatisfaction with your service, your contract of employment will be terminated in accordance with statutory regulations.

If you feel that any disciplinary action taken against you or that the termination of your contract has been unfair, you have the right to appeal to the managing director who will review all the circumstances of your appeal and his decision in the matter will be final.

If you have any grievances relating to your employment with the Company, you should discuss the matter with your manager. If the matter is not satisfactorily resolved, you have the right to approach the managing director who will make the final decision.

I ACKNOWLEDGE RECEIPT OF THE ABOVE STATEMENT

....

Signature of employee

....

Date

Appendix 7

Statutory Rights of Employees

Provided by the Employment Protection (Consolidation) Act 1978, Race Relations Act 1976, Sex Discrimination Act 1975

Period of continuous service after which the statutory right takes effect*	Employee's statutory right
Pre-employment	Discrimination – the right to be afforded equal access to employment regardless of sex, race or marital status.
On commencement of employment	The right not to be unlawfully discriminated against in employment on the grounds of sex, race, or marital status.
	The right to receive a Statement of Terms and Conditions of Employment within 13 weeks.
	The right to receive an itemised pay statement (ie gross pay, PAYE, NI etc)
	The right not to have unlawful deductions made from wages or salaries.
	The right not to be dismissed or have action short of dismissal taken against you for:
	(a) being or refusing to be a member of an independent trade union
	(b) taking part in the activities of an independent trade union.
	The right to reasonable time off to carry out:
	(a) Trade union duties (paid)
	(b) Trade union activities (unpaid)
	(c) Public duties (unpaid)

* A week during which an employee is employed under a contract of employment for more than 16 hours per week counts towards continuous service.

The right of access to data held on computer of which the employee is the subject and the right to seek compensation for damages caused by the loss, destruction or unauthorised disclosure of data, or by inaccurate data.

After one month

The right to receive a Guarantee Payment for up to five days when an employer is unable to provide work in any three-month period. This payment is limited to a maximum of £11.30 per day.

The right to receive up to 26 weeks' pay if the employee is suspended from work on medical grounds.

On termination of employment by the employer, an employee is entitled to receive one week's paid notice.

After six months

If dismissed, the right to receive a written statement of the reason for dismissal.

After two years

The right to receive maternity pay and the right to return to work after the birth of the baby.

The employee's paid notice entitlement increases to one week for each full year of employment, to a maximum of 12 weeks.

The right not to be unfairly dismissed.

The right to receive a redundancy payment if the employer's requirement for an employee to carry out work of a particular kind ceases or diminishes.

Appendix 8

Specimen Management Accounts

Profit and Loss Account Month ....

		Budget £	Month Actual £	Variance £	Budget £	Cumulative Actual £	Variance £
Sales	A	___	___	___	___	___	___
Opening stock							
Add:							
Purchases							
Less:							
Closing stock		___	___	___	___	___	___
Cost of sales	B	___	___	___	___	___	___
Gross profit (A–B)	C						
Gross profit % (C/A × 100)							
Overheads							
Salaries and wages							
Directors' remuneration							
Depreciation							
Light, heat and power							
Repairs and renewals							
Rent and rates							
Travelling and entertaining							
Bank interest and charges							
Advertising							
General expenses		___	___	___	___	___	___
Total overheads	D	___	___	___	___	___	___
Net profit (C–D)	E	═══	═══	═══	═══	═══	═══

Net profit % (E/A × 100%)

Balance Sheet Month End ....

	Budget £	Actual £	Variance £
FIXED ASSETS			
Freehold/leasehold property			
Motor vehicles			
Plant and machinery			
	___	___	___
Less:			
Depreciation			
	___	___	___
A			
	___	___	___
CURRENT ASSETS			
Stock and work in progress			
Debtors			
Cash at bank and in hand			
	___	___	___
B			
	___	___	___
CURRENT LIABILITIES			
Creditors			
Bank overdraft			
	___	___	___
C			
	___	___	___
NET CURRENT ASSETS (B–C) D			
LIABILITIES PAYABLE IN MORE THAN ONE YEAR (eg bank loans) E			
	___	___	___
NET ASSETS (A+D–E) F			
	══	══	══
Representing:			
Share capital/			
Proprietors' undrawn profit			
Profit retained in business			
	___	___	___
SHAREHOLDERS'/ PROPRIETORS' FUNDS G			
	══	══	══

[Note that F=G]

Cash Flow for the Month ....

	Budget		Actual	
	£	£	£	£

Balance at the beginning of the month
Add:

Receipts:	Sales	
	Sundry receipts	
	Other (specify)	

Less:
Payments:
Purchases
Directors' remuneration
Employees' salaries and wages
PAYE
VAT
Light, heat and power
Repairs and renewals
Rent and rates
Travelling and entertaining
Bank interest and charges
Advertising
General expenses
Capital expenditure
Other (specify)

Balance at the end of the month   £   £

Appendix 9
Useful Contacts and Addresses

Please note that the London telephone area code changes on 6 May 1990, and 01 will become either 071 (central area) or 081.

1. Accountants
The Institute of Chartered Accountants in England and Wales
399 Silbury Boulevard
Central Milton Keynes MK9 2HL
0908 668833

The Chartered Association of Certified Accountants
29 Lincoln's Inn Fields
London WC2A 3EE
01-242 6855

The Chartered Institute of Management Accountants
63 Portland Place
London W1N 4AB
01-637 2311

The Institute of Chartered Accountants of Scotland
27 Queen Street
Edinburgh EH2 1LA
031-225 5673

The Institute of Chartered Accountants in Ireland
Chartered Accountants House
87–89 Pembroke Road
Dublin 4
Dublin 680400

2. Solicitors
The Law Society
113 Chancery Lane
London WC2A 1PL
01-242 1222

3. Banks

Barclays Bank plc
54 Lombard Street
London EC3P 3AH
01-626 1567

Lloyds Bank plc
71 Lombard Street
London EC3P 3BS
01-626 1500

Midland Bank plc
Poultry
London EC2P 2BX
01-260 8000

National Westminster Bank plc
21 Lombard Street
London EC3P 3AR
01-280 4444

The Royal Bank of Scotland plc
67 Lombard Street
London EC3P 3DL
01-623 4356

Trustee Savings Bank plc
235–241 Union Street
London SE1 0LR
01-633 9344

Allied Irish Banks plc
12 Old Jewry
London EC2R 8DP
01-606 4900

Co-operative Bank plc
78–80 Cornhill
London EC3V 3NJ
01-626 6543

National Girobank
10 Milk Street
London EC2V 8JH
01-600 6020

Chartered Institute of Bankers
10 Lombard Street
London EC3V 9AS
01-623 3531

4. Local Authorities
From your local telephone book

5. Rural Development Commission
(previously Council for Small Industries in Rural Areas)
141 Castle Street
Salisbury
Wiltshire SP1 3TP
0722 336255

Also:

The Rural Development Commission
11 Cowley Street
London SW1P 3NA
01-276 6969

6. Development Agencies and Boards (Regional)
Department of Trade and Industry
Regional Policy Support
66–74 Victoria Street
London SW1E 6SJ
01-215 7877

Or see your local telephone directory

7. Small Firms Service
Dial 100 and ask for Freefone Enterprise

8. English Estates
St George's House
Kingsway
Team Valley
Gateshead
Tyne and Wear NE11 0NA
091-487 8941

9. New Towns
Commission for the New Towns
Glen House
Stag Place
London SW1E 5AJ
01-828 7722

10. Urban Development Corporations

Black Country Development Corporation
Black Country House
Round Green Road
Oldbury
West Midlands B69 2NG
021-511 200

Bristol Development Corporation
2nd Floor
Techo House
Redcliffe Way
Bristol BS1 6NX
0272 255222

Central Manchester Development Corporation
Churchgate House
56 Oxford Street
Manchester M1 6EU
061-236 1166

Cleveland Development Corporation
Tees House
High Force Road
Riverside Park
Middlesbrough
Cleveland TS2 1RE
0642 230636

Leeds Development Corporation
5th Floor, South Point
South Accommodation Road
Leeds LS10 1WP
0532 446273

London Docklands Development Corporation
Unit A
Great Eastern Enterprise
Mill Harbour
London E14 9TJ
01-515 3000

Merseyside Development Corporation
Royal Liver Building
Pier Head
Liverpool L3 1JH
051-236 6090

Sheffield Development Corporation
Don Valley House
Savile Street East
Sheffield S4 7UQ
0742 720100

Trafford Park Development Corporation
Trafford Wharf Road
Trafford Park
Manchester M17 1EX
061-848 8000

Tyne and Wear Development Corporation
Hadrian House
Higham Place
Newcastle upon Tyne NE1 8AF
091-222 1222

11. Freeports

Belfast Airport
Northern Ireland Airports Ltd
Belfast

International Airport
Belfast BT29 4AB
08494 22888 (Ext 203)

Birmingham Airport
West Midlands Freeport Ltd
Birmingham Airport
Coventry Road
Birmingham B26 3QD
021-782 0103

Cardiff Port
Pearce (Wales) Ltd
15–16 Herbert Street
Cardiff CF1 5QS
0272 236500

Liverpool Port
Mersey Docks and Harbour Co
Port of Liverpool Building
Pier Head
Liverpool L3 1BZ
051-200 2173

Prestwick Airport
Freeport Scotland Ltd
Burns House
Burns Statue Square
Ayr KA7 1UT
0292 281511

Southampton Free Trade Zone Ltd
Southampton Free Trade Zone
Southampton SO1 0HJ
0703 335995

12. Enterprise Agencies
For details of your Local Enterprise Agency contact:

Business in the Community
227a City Road
London EC1V 1LX
01-253 3716

Scottish Business in the Community
Romano House
43 Station Road
Edinburgh EH12 7AF
031-334 9876

13. Chambers of Commerce
For details of your local Chamber of Commerce contact:

Association of British Chambers of Commerce:
Sovereign House
212a Shaftesbury Avenue
London WC2H 8EW
01-240 5831

14. New Enterprise Programme
The Training Agency
London Business School
Sussex Place
Regent's Park
London NW1 4SA
01-262 5050

Regional addresses:

Information Office
236 Gray's Inn Road
London WC1X 8HL
01-278 0363

15. Enterprise Allowance Scheme
Your local Jobcentre before start-up

16. Advertising
Advertising Association
Abford House
15 Wilton Road
London SW1V 1NJ
01-828 2771

17. Market research
Export Market Information Centre
Department of Trade and Industry
1 Victoria Street
London SW1H 0ET
01-215 5444

18. Exporting
British Exporters Association
16 Dartmouth Street
London SW1H 9BL
01-222 5419

British Overseas Trade Board
1 Victoria Street
London SW1H 0ET
01-215 7877

(Or nearest BOTB regional office)

Technical Help for Exporters
Linford Wood
Milton Keynes MK14 6LE
0908 220022

Institute of Export
64 Clifton Street
London EC2A 4MB
01-247 9812

Export Credits Guarantee Department
Export House
50 Ludgate Hill
London EC4M 7AY
01-382 7000

19. Europe

Liaison Office for the UK
European Investment Bank
68 Pall Mall
London SW1Y 5ES
01-839 3351

European Coal and Steel Community
The Directorate of Credit and Investments
Commission of European Communities
Bâtiment Jean Monnet
Kirchberg
Luxembourg
010-352 43011

20. Enterprise Zones

General information:

Department of the Environment
2 Marsham Street
London SW1P 3EB
01-212 4077

21. Venture capital

British Venture Capital Association
c/o Arthur Andersen & Co
1 Surrey Street
London WC2R 2PS
01-836 5702

22. Department of Trade and Industry

Regional Telephone numbers for advice on innovation, investment, exports and other help:

London 01-215 7877
North East 091-232 4722
East Midlands 0602 506181
North West 061-838 5000
South East 01-730 9678
South West 0272 272666
West Midlands 021-631 6181
Yorkshire and Humberside 0532 443171
Scotland 041-248 4774
Wales 0222 823185
Northern Ireland 0232 233233

23. ACAS
Advisory Conciliation and Arbitration Service
Clifton House
83–117 Euston Road
London NW1 2RB
01-388 5100

24. Patents
Chartered Institute of Patent Agents
Staple Inn Buildings
High Holborn
London WC1V 7PZ
01-405 9450

25. Limited company information, formation and searches
Companies House
Crown Way
Maindy
Cardiff CF4 3UZ
0222 388588

100 George Street
Edinburgh EH2 3DJ
031-225 5774

Chichester House
43–47 Chichester Court
Belfast BT1 4PJ
0232 234121

London Search Room
Companies House
55–71 City Road
London EC1V 1BB
01-253 9393

Or most Company Registration Agents from the Yellow Pages

26. Factoring
Association of British Factors
24–28 Bloomsbury Way
London WC1A 2PX
01-831 4268

27. Franchising
The British Franchise Association
Thames View
Newtown Road
Henley on Thames
Oxon RG9 1HG
0491 578049

28. General
Association of Self-employed People
279 Church Road
London SE19 2QQ
01-653 4798

29. Wages Councils
Head Office
The Office of Wages Councils
Steel House
11 Tothill Street
London SW1H 9NF
01-273 4808

Regional Offices

The Department of Employment
Wages Inspectorate
Cumberland House
200 Broad Street
Birmingham B15 1TD
021-631 3300

The Wages Inspectorate
Fifth Floor
125 Queens Road
Brighton BN1 3WB
0273 23333

The Wages Inspectorate
Department of Employment
Seventh Floor
The Pithay
Bristol BS1 2NQ
0272 273710

The Wages Inspectorate
First Floor
Lord Alexandra House
Waterhouse Street
Hemel Hempstead
Hertfordshire HP1 1DW

The Wages Inspectorate
Room 309
City House
Leeds LS1 4JH
0532 438232

The Wages Inspectorate
Clifton House
83–117 Euston Road
London NW1 2RA
01-387 2511

Department of Employment
The Wages Inspectorate
c/o Broadacre House
Market Street East
Newcastle upon Tyne NE1 6HQ
091-232 1881

Department of Employment
The Wages Inspectorate
127–129 George Street
Edinburgh EH2 4JH
031-220 2777

30. Regional contacts for the Enterprise Initiative
DTI North-East
Cleveland, Durham
Northumberland, Tyne and Wear
Consultancy Initiatives:
091-235 7292
Other Initiatives: 091-232 4722
Stanegate House
2 Groat Market
Newcastle upon Tyne NE1 1YN

DTI North-West (Manchester)
Cheshire (except Chester)
Cumbria, Lancashire, Greater
Manchester and the High Peak
District of Derbyshire
All Initiatives: 061-838 5000
75 Mosley Street
Manchester M2 3HR

DTI North-West (Liverpool)
Liverpool, Widnes/Runcorn
Wirral/Chester, and St Helens/
Wigan
All Initiatives: 051-224 6300
Graeme House
Derby Square
Liverpool L2 7UP

DTI Yorkshire and Humberside
North Yorkshire, South Yorkshire
West Yorkshire and Humberside
Consultancy Initiatives:
Leeds (0532) 338 300
Regional Enterprise Grants:
(0532) 338 360
Other Initiatives: 0532 443 171
Priestley House
3–5 Park Row
Leeds LS1 5LF

DTI East Midlands
Nottinghamshire, Derbyshire
(except the High Peak District)
Leicestershire, Lincolnshire and
Northamptonshire
Consultancy Initiatives:
Nottingham (0602) 596 460
Regional Enterprise Grants:
Northampton (0604) 21051 ext 35
Other Initiatives: (0602) 506 181
Severns House
20 Middle Pavement
Nottingham NG1 7DW

DTI West Midlands
Formerly West Midlands
Metropolitan County, Hereford
and Worcester, Shropshire,
Staffordshire and Warwickshire
All Initiatives: 021-631 6181
Ladywood House
Stephenson Street
Birmingham B2 4DT

DTI South-East (London)
Greater London, Kent, Surrey,
Sussex
Consultancy Initiatives:
01-627 7800
Other Initiatives: 01-730 9678
Bridge Place
88–89 Eccleston Square
London SW1V 1PT

DTI South-East (Cambridge)
Bedfordshire, Cambridgeshire,
Essex, Hertfordshire, Norfolk,
Suffolk
All initiatives:
Cambridge (0223) 461 939
The Westbrook Centre
Milton Road
Cambridge CB4 1YG

DTI South-East (Reading)
Berkshire, Buckinghamshire,
Hampshire, Oxfordshire and
Isle of Wight
All Initiatives: Reading (0734) 395 600
40 Caversham Road
Reading, Berkshire

DTI South-West
Avon, Cornwall (including Isles
of Scilly), Devon, Dorset,
Gloucestershire, Somerset and
Wiltshire
Consultancy Initiatives:
Bristol (0272) 308 400
Regional Enterprise Grants:
Penzance (0736) 60440
Other Initiatives: (0272) 272 666
The Pithay
Bristol BS1 2PB

Scotland: Scottish Office
All Initiatives: 041-248 4774
Industry Department of Scotland
Alhambra House
Waterloo Street
Glasgow G2 6AT

Wales: Welsh Office
Consultancy Initiatives: (0443) 841777
(24 hours) or if you live in
Mid Wales Dial 100 and ask for
Freefone New Wales
Other Initiatives: (0222) 823185 (24 hours)
Welsh Office Industry Department
New Crown Building
Cathays Park
Cardiff CF1 3NQ

Further Reading from Kogan Page

Kogan Page publish an extensive list of books for small and medium-sized businesses; those particularly helpful to the reader of this book are likely to be:

Be Your Own Company Secretary, A J Scrine, 1987

Business Rip-Offs and How to Avoid Them, Tony Attwood, 1987

Buying for Business, Tony Attwood, 1988

Don't Do. Delegate! James M Jenks and John M Kelly, 1986

Effective Advertising: The Daily Telegraph Guide for the Small Business, H C Carter, 1986

The Entrepreneur's Complete Self-Assessment Guide, Douglas A Gray, 1987

Export for the Small Business, 2nd Edition, Henry Deschampsneufs, 1988

Financial Management for the Small Business, 2nd Edition, Colin Barrow, 1988

Getting Sales: A Practical Guide to Getting More Sales for Your Business, R D Smith and G M Dick, 1986

Good Franchise Guide, The, 2nd Edition, Tony Attwood and Len Hough, 1989

How To Be an Even Better Manager, Michael Armstrong, 1988

How to Buy a Business: The Daily Telegraph Guide, 2nd Edition, Peter Farrell, 1989

How to Choose Business Premises: A Guide for the Small Firm, Howard Green, Brian Chalkley and Paul Foley, 1986

How to Promote Your Own Business, Jim Dudley, 1987

Importing for the Small Business: The Daily Telegraph Guide, 2nd Edition, Mag Morris, 1988

Law for the Small Business: The Daily Telegraph Guide, 6th edition, Patricia Clayton, 1988

The Practice of Successful Business Management, Kenneth Winckles, 1986

Raising Finance: The Guardian Guide for the Small Business, 3rd edition, Clive Woodcock, 1989

Start and Run a Profitable Consultancy, Douglas A Gray, 1989

The Stoy Hayward Business Tax Guide, Mavis Seymour and Stephen Say (annual)

Successful Expansion for the Small Business: The Daily Telegraph Guide, M J Morris, 1984

Successful Marketing for the Small Business: The Daily Telegraph Guide, 2nd Edition, Dave Patten, 1989

Taking Up a Franchise: The Daily Telegraph Guide, 6th edition, Colin Barrow and Godfrey Golzen, 1989

Index